# Alicia's Beginner Cookbook

## Minute-by-Minute

*For Bob, Melissa and Patricia with love*

*Acknowledgements: Drawings by Patricia Reynolds, Editing by Jerry O'Connor*

**ISBN 9781452806556**

*Printed in the United States of America*

*FIRST EDITION*

# Contents

# *Introduction*

An important goal of mine in writing this book is to share some discoveries I made when I first began cooking. The way our society works these days, cooking at home for individuals or families is discouraged. We believe we do not have much time to do anything, and cooking falls low on our list of priorities. Many of us are being raised without any instruction or background in food preparation.

As a result, the whole endeavor can be a real "pain in the petunias" if you lack experience. On the other hand, if you approach it properly and are well organized and prepared, cooking can be very enjoyable and not that hard to attack.

Over the many years I've been cooking, I have raised preparation of my meals to a comfortable level through trial and error. When you are first greeted by instructions in a cookbook, you are usually confronted with only minimal data. This may lead to misunderstandings about how to best follow an individual recipe, which can spoil preparation of an entire meal. As time goes on, you move forward with experience in cooking, and many of us eventually establish our own cooking routines and comfortable systems. This book can benefit any cook. I hope to help beginning cooks here, most of all, but intermediates may also find something they enjoy.

All of these meals can be prepared at a low cost. The recipes presented here have worked well within budgeting I established while cooking for my family. Many times we wish to plan and cook simple, inexpensive, and nutritious meals for an entire week. I have set out to accomplish just that.

I will be demonstrating my method of organizing the preparation of entire meals, along with tips and shortcuts I've learned over the years. As you will see, my meals all have a main entrée, a vegetable, and a carbohydrate plate on the side. I want to save you from experiencing many of the blunders I underwent in my cooking endeavors, so I will help you make best use of your meal preparation time.

Each recipe has a designated time allotment for every step involved in preparing a recipe and, very importantly, will help you to complete and serve everything at the same time. The minutes at the left of each step indicate the time needed to accomplish each step. For example, in the very first recipe, Apricot Chicken Noodle, one of the timed steps indicates 4 minutes needed for "Fill a pot with water ..." and another 3 minutes for "Rinse and chop green onions". Total completion time, which is total time for all the steps, will be noted at the top of each recipe.

I have found that most of the time I prepare vegetables or pasta dishes, individuals garnish meals with KRAFT grated Parmesan cheese for added flavoring. This is a tasty adornment that can be added in the amount desired by the person. I suggest the container be placed at the dinner table for easy access! In preparing these meals, I have also estimated the proper amount of spices, such as salt and pepper. However, you can adjust them to suite your individual tastes.

I find it very practical to organize meals for the upcoming week ahead of time by selecting a full set of recipes. I can usually limit my trips to the grocery store to just one per week, which relieves a lot of stress caused by more frequent visits. Toward the end of the book, I included a sample grocery list I compiled from my own shopping trips. The general supplies in this list will accommodate you for about two months, and the food items will remind you of things to buy when you review your weekly needs.

An important factor necessary to easing your cooking endeavor is to make an inventory of the cooking utensils you own and note any updating you may need to do. Your upgrades should be based on the kind of cooking you like to do. I will share with you a list of necessities I keep in my kitchen for cooking.

Another practical thing to keep in mind is what you can do with shortcuts to save yourself time without shortchanging your meal. Remember, the meals you prepare must be appealing to those for whom you cook, or they may not be appreciated and might not even be consumed. The recipes shown here are well-liked and usually very popular.

Four recipes in this cookbook require some special treatment. These use a cooking tool called a "dry cooker". This is a large covered pan with a raised platform vent. Hot air gases give the meat a great charred taste, which I believe enhances the taste of the meat. If you do not have a dry cooker, a large covered frying pan can be used, although the charred flavoring may not be attained. The Dry Cooker recipes are: Beef and Noodles, Chicken and Mushrooms, Dry Cooker Chicken Strips, and Walnut Chicken Strips.

## Alicia's Minute-by-Minute Meals in Cooking Time Order
### Cooking Time is presented as Hour: Minutes

| Cooking Time | Recipe Title | Page |
|---|---|---|
| 0:20 | Martian Food | 66 |
| 0:25 | Apricot Chicken Noodle | 15 |
| 0:25 | Beef & Noodles in a Dry Cooker | 46 |
| 0:25 | Bird's Eye Broccoli Stir-Fry | 76 |
| 0:30 | Beef Italiano | 45 |
| 0:33 | Orientalized Beef | 54 |
| 0:40 | Springtime Spaghetti | 75 |
| 0:40 | Sirloin Burger Stroganoff | 56 |
| 0:45 | Curry Chicken | 23 |
| 0:45 | Spaghetti | 58 |
| 0:48 | Sirloin Steak Stroganoff | 55 |
| 0:50 | Easy Beef Chuck Mix | 60 |
| 0:50 | Chicken Noodle Dinner | 19 |
| 0:50 | Crispy Italian Eggplant & Brussels Sprouts | 73 |
| 0:50 | Chicken in Mellow White Cream Sauce | 20 |
| 0:55 | Pasta with Turkey Sausage & Tomatoes | 68 |
| 0:55 | Quick Italian Chicken | 37 |
| 0:55 | Cheesy Corn Tortilla Bake | 72 |
| 0:55 | Walnut Chicken Strips in a Dry Cooker | 43 |
| 0:55 | Dry Cooker Chicken Strips with Vegetable Stir-Fry | 26 |
| 0:56 | Chicken & Mushrooms in a Dry Cooker with Chinese Style Vegetables | 18 |
| 1:00 | Tuna Circle with Cheese Sauce & Water-Fried Broccoli | 70 |
| 1:00 | Meaty Halloween Lasagna Casserole | 51 |
| 1:00 | Rockfish with Chinese Style Vegetables & Low-Carb Pasta | 69 |
| 1:00 | Garam Marsala Chicken with Cheddar Garden Pasta | 28 |
| 1:10 | Noodle Casserole | 52 |
| 1:10 | Oriental Chicken & Grapes with Chinese Style Vegetables | 36 |
| 1:15 | Savory Baked Chicken Breasts | 38 |
| 1:15 | Spinach Soufflé | 74 |
| 1:15 | Sirloin Stew | 64 |
| 1:15 | Cheesy Chicken & Rice Bake | 16 |

| | | |
|---|---|---|
| 1:20 | Orange Bunny Chicken | 35 |
| 1:20 | Spicy Oven Chicken | 40 |
| 1:25 | Intoxicated Chicken | 30 |
| 1:25 | Tomato Rice Porcupines | 53 |
| 1:25 | Chicken Gone Wild! | 44 |
| 1:28 | Mushgush Quiche Lorraine | 67 |
| 1:40 | Chili | 50 |
| 2:00 | Smashed Potato Chicken Bowl | 32 |
| 2:00 | Crunched Chicken Strips | 24 |
| 2:05 | Lasagna | 48 |
| 3:05 | Lemon Honey Chicken | 34 |
| 4:10 | Pot Roast | 62 |
| 5:30 | Thai Chicken in a Crock Pot | 42 |
| 6:00 | Chicken Chop Suey in a Crock Pot | 17 |
| 6:00 | Spanish Beer Chicken in a Crock Pot | 39 |
| 6:00 | California Pilaf in a Crock Pot | 47 |
| 8:00 | Chicken Tetrazzini in a Crock Pot | 21 |
| 8:30 | Coq au Vin in a Crock Pot | 22 |
| 8:30 | Ham & Scalloped Potatoes in a Crock Pot | 65 |
| 9:59 | Italianized Chicken with a Spicy Kick in a Crock Pot | 29 |

# *Alicia's Minute-by-Minute Meals in Alphabetical Order*

| Recipe Title | Cooking Time | Page |
|---|---|---|
| Apricot Chicken Noodle | 0:25 | 15 |
| Beef & Noodles in a Dry Cooker | 0:25 | 46 |
| Beef Italiano | 0:30 | 45 |
| California Pilaf in a Crock Pot | 6:20 | 47 |
| Cheesy Chicken & Rice Bake | 1:15 | 16 |
| Cheesy Corn Tortilla Bake | 0:55 | 72 |
| Chicken Chop Suey in a Crock Pot | 6:00 | 17 |
| Chicken Gone Wild! | 1:25 | 44 |
| Chicken in Mellow White Cream Sauce | 0:50 | 20 |
| Chicken & Mushrooms in a Dry Cooker with Chinese Style Vegetables | 0:56 | 18 |
| Chicken Noodle Dinner | 0:50 | 19 |
| Chicken Tetrazzini in a Crock Pot | 8:00 | 21 |
| Chili | 1:40 | 50 |
| Coq au Vin in a Crock Pot | 8:30 | 22 |
| Crispy Italian Eggplant & Brussels Sprouts | 0:50 | 73 |
| Crunched Chicken Strips | 2:00 | 24 |
| Curry Chicken | 0:45 | 23 |
| Dry Cooker Chicken Strips with Vegetable Stir-Fry | 0:55 | 26 |
| Easy Beef Chuck Mix | 0:50 | 60 |
| Garam Marsala Chicken with Cheddar Garden Pasta | 1:00 | 28 |
| Ham & Scalloped Potatoes in a Crock Pot | 8:30 | 65 |
| Intoxicated Chicken | 1:25 | 30 |
| Italianized Chicken with a Spicy Kick in a Crock Pot | 10:00 | 29 |
| Lasagna | 2:05 | 48 |
| Lemon Honey Chicken | 3:05 | 34 |
| Martian Food | 0:20 | 66 |
| Meaty Halloween Lasagna Casserole | 1:00 | 51 |
| Mushgush Quiche Lorraine | 1:28 | 67 |
| Noodle Casserole | 1:10 | 52 |
| Orange Bunny Chicken | 1:20 | 35 |
| Oriental Chicken & Grapes with Chinese Style Vegetables | 1:10 | 36 |
| Orientalized Beef | 0:33 | 54 |
| Pasta with Turkey Sausage & Tomatoes | 0:55 | 68 |
| Pot Roast | 4:10 | 62 |
| Quick Italian Chicken | 0:55 | 37 |

| | | |
|---|---|---|
| Rockfish with Chinese Style Vegetables & Low-Carb Pasta | 1:00 | 69 |
| Savory Baked Chicken Breasts | 1:15 | 38 |
| Sirloin Steak Stroganoff | 0:48 | 55 |
| Sirloin Burger Stroganoff | 0:40 | 56 |
| Sirloin Stew | 1:15 | 64 |
| Smashed Potato Chicken Bowl | 2:00 | 32 |
| Spaghetti | 0:45 | 58 |
| Spanish Beer Chicken in a Crock Pot | 6:00 | 39 |
| Spicy Oven Chicken | 1:20 | 40 |
| Spinach Soufflé | 1:15 | 74 |
| Springtime Spaghetti | 0:40 | 75 |
| Thai Chicken in a Crock Pot | 5:30 | 42 |
| Tomato Rice Porcupines | 1:25 | 53 |
| Tuna Circle with Cheese Sauce & Water-Fried Broccoli | 1:00 | 70 |
| Walnut Chicken Strips in a  Dry Cooker | 0:55 | 43 |

## *Vegetables*

| Recipe Title | Cooking Time | Page |
|---|---|---|
| Bird's Eye Broccoli Stir-Fry | 0:25 | 76 |
| Bok Choy | 0:12 | 77 |
| Broccoli | 0:15 | 77 |
| Brussels Sprouts | 0:20 | 77 |
| Brussels Sprouts & Carrots | 0:30 | 78 |
| Green Beans | 0:10 | 78 |
| Snow Peas & Carrots | 0:21 | 78 |

# *Menus*

## *Chicken*

### *Apricot Chicken Noodle* ☺
Chicken pieces (pre-cooked) stove-top prepared in a rich apricot sauce.
Served with bow-tie noodles. Water stir-fried green beans accompany.

### *Cheesy Chicken & Rice Bake* ☺
Boneless chicken breast pieces oven-baked in a cream of chicken soup, with
rice, onion, and cheddar cheese. Served with water stir-fried green beans.

### *Chicken Chop Suey in a Crock Pot*
Full crock pot entree of chicken chop suey with celery, mushrooms, and bean
sprouts. Served with brown rice and water stir-fried broccoli.

### *Chicken Gone Wild!* ☺
Oven-baked chicken casserole flavored with onion and cream of mushroom soup.
Long grain and wild rice is included in preparation. Served alongside with water
stir-fried green beans.

### *Chicken in Mellow White Cream Sauce* ☺
Stove-top chicken dinner in thick sauce of white wine, chicken broth,
and cream. Served over low-carb pasta.  Start off with a dinner salad.

### *Chicken & Mushrooms in a Dry Cooker with Chinese Style Vegetables* ☺ ☺
Chicken breasts cooked in dry cooker with mushroom cheese sauce.
Served with brown rice and Chinese Style Vegetables.

### *Chicken Noodle Dinner*
Chicken casserole oven dish, combined with multiple vegetables and
Fettuccine Alfredo. Start off with a dinner salad.

### *Chicken Tetrazzini  in a Crock Pot* ☺ ☺
Crock pot chicken dish thickened with mushrooms, cream of mushroom
soup, and chicken broth. Served over low-carb pasta.  Accompanied by water
stir-fried broccoli.

### Coq au Vin in a Crock Pot
Crock pot chicken dinner using red wine, bacon crumbs, and many spices. Small potatoes are included in the meal. Accompanied by water stir-fried broccoli.

### Crunched Chicken Strips
Oven-baked marinated chicken breast strips. Served with smashed potatoes and water stir-fried broccoli.

### Curry Chicken ☺
Stove-top chicken recipe served with white rice and water stir-fried broccoli.

### Dry Cooker Chicken Strips with Vegetable Stir-Fry ☺
Chicken strips cooked in dry cooker, served with Teriyaki sauce. Accompanied by brown rice and multiple stir-fried vegetables.

### Garam Marsala Chicken with Cheddar Garden Pasta ☺
Chicken breasts marinated in Indian seasoning of Garam Marsala are oven-baked, served with corkscrew pasta and cooked carrot slices.

### Intoxicated Chicken ☺ ☺
Chicken breasts oven-baked in white wine with onion pieces and garlic powder. Served with smashed potatoes and water stir-fried broccoli.

### Italianized Chicken with a Spicy Kick in a Crock Pot ☺
Chicken breasts prepared with Italian stewed tomatoes - cooked in crock pot. Served with low-carb pasta and water stir-fried broccoli.

### Lemon Honey Chicken
Boneless chicken breasts marinated in lemon honey sauce are oven-baked. Served with brown rice and water stir-fried broccoli.

### Smashed Potato Chicken Bowl ☺ ☺ ☺
Oven-baked bowl made with a mixture of smashed potatoes, cheese and crispy *Durkee's® French Fried Onions* - serving a blend of pre-cooked chicken breasts, mixed vegetables, Cream of Chicken Soup, and assorted spices. This is escorted by a salad.

### Orange Bunny Chicken ☺
Chicken breasts oven-baked in rich orange juice sauce and carrots. Served with egg noodles and salad.

***Oriental Chicken & Grapes with Chinese Style Vegetables*** ☺ ☺
Oven-baked chicken breasts with Oriental flavoring including honey and soy sauce. Served with brown rice and water stir-fried Chinese style vegetables.

***Quick Italian Chicken*** ☺ ☺
Boneless oven-baked cheesy chicken breasts cooked in Italian tomato-based sauce. Served with brown rice and water stir-fried green beans.

***Savory Baked Chicken Breasts*** ☺
Oven-baked chicken breasts covered with a flavorful baked-on bread crumb crust. Served with baked potatoes and water stir-fried green beans.

***Spanish Beer Chicken in a Crock Pot*** ☺ ☺
Chicken breast pieces cooked in a crock pot with tomato paste/beer sauce and stuffed green olives, and seasoned with garlic. This is accompanied by brown rice and water stir-fried green beans.

***Spicy Oven Chicken*** ☺
Oven-baked chicken breasts flavored with spicy flour coating. Served with smashed potatoes and steamed cauliflower.

***Thai Chicken in a Crock Pot***
Chicken breasts enriched with flavoring of coconut milk, green onions, ginger, red pepper flakes, turmeric, and pineapple chunks. Served with brown rice and accompanied by water stir-fried broccoli.

***Walnut Chicken Strips in a Dry Cooker*** ☺
Chicken strips cooked in dry cooker with vegetables, flavored with barbecue sauce. Served with brown rice and salad.

# *Ground Beef*

### *Beef Italiano*
Ground beef browned and cooked with red and green bell peppers,
onion wedges, and Italian stewed tomatoes. Served with low-carb pasta.
Water stir-fried green beans accompany.

### *Beef & Noodles in a Dry Cooker* ☺
Ground sirloin beef browned in dry cooker with chopped onion,
and richly flavored with cream of mushroom soup. Served with egg noodles.
Accompanied by water stir-fried broccoli.

### *California Pilaf in a Crock Pot* ☺ ☺
Crock Pot prepared California Pilaf Meal made with lean ground beef, including
rice in the meal. Served with a salad.

### *Chili* ☺ ☺ ☺
Flavorful pot of ground beef chili. Served with a salad.

### *Meaty Halloween Lasagna Casserole*
Thick and simple-to-prepare oven-baked ground beef lasagna enriched with
cheddar cheese and topped with sour cream. Served with a salad.

### *Lasagna*
Oven-baked ground beef lasagna entree rich in Italian flavoring with Parmesan,
Mozzarella, and cottage cheeses. Served with a salad.

### *Noodle Casserole*
Oven-baked ground beef tomato noodle casserole enriched with cottage and
cheddar cheeses. Accompanied by water stir-fried broccoli.

### *Orientalized Beef*
Stove-top Orientalized ground beef browned and cooked in multiple vegetables.
Served with low-carb pasta and a salad.

### *Sirloin Burger Stroganoff* ☺
Ground sirloin steak browned with mushrooms and onions. Rich stroganoff
sauce of multi-spices and cream of chicken soup. Served with whole wheat
grain pasta and multi vegetable/bok choy stir-fry.

### Spaghetti ☺
Flavorful browned ground beef spaghetti sauce. Served with Capellini pasta and salad.

### Tomato Rice Porcupines
Ground beef meatballs - rolled with uncooked white rice - oven-baked with Worcestershire spiced garlic tomato sauce. Accompanied by water stir-fried green beans.

# Beef

### Sirloin Steak Stroganoff
Made with sirloin steak strips, richly flavored sauce. Served with Dutch noodles. Accompanied by water stir-fried broccoli.

### Easy Beef Chuck Mix
Beef chuck cubes stove-top cooked in onion slices and garlic with spicy Worcestershire sauce. Served over Dutch egg noodles. Accompanied by water stir-fried green beans.

### Pot Roast ☺
Oven-baked Pot Roast Dinner served with smashed potatoes and water stir-fried broccoli.

### Sirloin Stew
Stove-top stew feasting sirloin beef, potatoes, Italian tomatoes, bell pepper, and petite green peas. Accompanied by a salad.

# Deli Meat

### Ham & Scalloped Potatoes in a Crock Pot
Crock pot entree made with deli luncheon meat ham. Water stir-fried green beans accompany.

### Martian Food ☺ ☺
Stove-top entree made with deli luncheon meat ham, cream of celery soup, peas, and mushrooms. Served over spinach fettuccine noodles. Accompanied by salad.

### Mushgush Quiche Lorraine ☺ ☺ ☺
Deli luncheon meat ham sauce made with eggs, whipping cream, and spices cooked in a deep dish pie crust. Water stir-fried green beans accompany.

### Pasta with Turkey Sausage & Tomatoes ☺
Stove-top browned turkey sausage slices cooked in thick Italianized tomato sauce. Served over Rotini pasta and accompanied by water stir-fried broccoli.

## Miscellaneous Seafood

### Rockfish with Chinese Style Vegetables & Low-Carb Pasta ☺
Oven-baked Rockfish fillets served with low-carb pasta and Chinese Style veggies.

### Tuna Circle with Cheese Sauce & Water-Fried Broccoli
Oven-baked Tuna Circle served with a rich Cheddar cheese sauce. Accompanied by water stir-fried broccoli.

## Tortilla Bake and Vegetarian Dishes

### Cheesy Corn Tortilla Bake ☺ ☺
Corn tortilla slices are oven-baked with jack cheese, corn, and green onions. The dish is doused with an egg and buttermilk mixture, and flavored with chili peppers. Served with brown rice and barbecued beans. Accompanied by a salad.

### Crispy Italian Eggplant & Brussels Sprouts
Oven-baked eggplant slices are topped with meatless spaghetti sauce and served with pasta. Accompanied by Brussels sprouts boiled with onion rings in chicken broth.

### Spinach Soufflé
Easy, oven-baked Spinach Soufflé rich in cheddar and cottage cheeses. Accompanied by a salad.

### Springtime Spaghetti ☺
Multiple stir-fried vegetables topped by a creamy sauce rich in Parmesan cheese are served over spaghettini noodles. Accompanied by a salad.

## *Vegetable Cooking*

Bird's Eye Broccoli Stir-Fry
Bok Choy
Broccoli
Brussels Sprouts

Brussels Sprouts & Carrots
Green Beans
Snow Peas & Carrots

# Recipes

## Apricot Chicken Noodle

**Apricots in the recipe give a sweet twist to this stove-top chicken dinner served with bow-tie noodles. Green beans give a simple and quick accompaniment. Total completion time: 28 minutes**

- ❖ *3 large chicken breasts pre-cooked*
- ❖ *6 green onions*
- ❖ *1½ cups half & half cream*
- ❖ *1 lb. green beans*
- ❖ *2 tbsp. salted butter*

- ❖ *Barilla® Fafalle Bow-tie noodles*
- ❖ *2 cans (17 oz. each) apricots, drained*
- ❖ *Kraft ® grated parmesan for flavoring of each individual plate*

**Minutes**

:04   Fill a pot with water to cook the noodles in. Bring to a boil. At the same time, slice chicken breasts, about 1½ inches thick and 2-4 inches long, removing all meat from bones. Smaller pieces are okay - no need to waste any chicken (just keep smaller pieces on top when putting in saucepan).

:03   Rinse and chop green onions.

:03   In a medium saucepan, simmer half & half cream for 3 minutes.

:03   Proceed to rinse and chop green beans.

:03   Add butter and chicken to saucepan with half & half cream. Cover and simmer 3 minutes.

:02   Add bow-tie noodles to water. Bring back to a boil and set timer for 12 minutes (or whatever time designated).

:01   Use a large frying pan to cook your green beans in. Preheat pan 1 minute. Add 2 tbsp. of water. Bring to a boil.

:04   Add green beans. Cover and maintain high heat.

:02   Add green onions and apricots to chicken.

:03   Green beans are now ready. Remove from heat and remove any remaining water.
Pasta is now ready. Remove and run hot water through noodles. Drain.
Treat your sweet tooth!!

*Tip* Chicken can be pre-cooked in a pot of boiling water. Keep fully covered with water, maintaining boiling water. Cook for 15 minutes. Make sure no meat is pink.

# *Cheesy Chicken & Rice Bake*

**Prep work for this menu is minimal and simple. Cheesiness makes this one quite appealing.  Total completion time: 1 hour and 16 minutes**

- ❖ *½ small onion*
- ❖ *3 large chicken breasts*
- ❖ *1 can of Campbell's® Cream of Chicken Soup*
- ❖ *½ cup of water*
- ❖ *1 lb. of green beans*

- ❖ *¾ cups Uncle Ben's® white rice*
- ❖ *¼ tsp. black pepper*
- ❖ *2 cups cheddar cheese*
- ❖ *½ tsp. Mrs. DASH® Salt Free Original Blend Seasoning*

**Minutes**

:03  Preheat oven to 375º. Mince the small onion.

:10  After rinsing the chicken breasts, remove all skin and excess fat. Then remove meat from bones, keeping pieces slices thin. Set aside.

:02  In a 2-quart shallow baking dish, mix soup, water, rice, onion pieces, black pepper, and seasoning.

:15  Cover with foil and place in oven for 15 minutes.

:35  Spread the chicken pieces covering the rice mixture with larger chicken pieces on top, and sprinkle more black pepper on top. Return to oven for 45 minutes, covered.  Use time now to shred cheddar cheese.
Proceed to rinse and chop green beans.

:02  Use a large frying pan to cook the green beans in. Preheat pan 1 minute. Add 2 tbsp. of water. Bring to a boil.

:05  Add green beans. Cover and cook while maintaining high heat for 5 minutes, add water if needed.

:01  Green beans are now done. Remove chicken from oven. Sprinkle cheddar cheese over entire spread.

:03  Return to oven for 3 minutes, uncovered.
Remove chicken from oven. Dinner is ready for you to attack!

# Chicken Chop Suey in a Crock Pot

One thing I found convenient about this crock pot dinner is that all ingredients, including chicken and vegetables, can be chopped prior to cooking (early in the day or the night before) and then refrigerated. Actual cooking time is 5 to 6 hours on low and then an additional 20 minutes on high.  Total completion time: 6 hours

- ❖ **1 cup water**
- ❖ **3 chicken breasts**
- ❖ **1 Herb ox chicken bouillon cube**
- ❖ **2 large celery stalks**
- ❖ **5 green onions**
- ❖ **1 tbsp. ground ginger**
- ❖ **¼ cup KIKKOMAN® Soy Sauce**

- ❖ **1 cup Mahatma brown rice**
- ❖ **1 crown of broccoli**
- ❖ **4 oz. fresh mushrooms**
- ❖ **4 oz. fresh bean sprouts**
- ❖ **1 tsp. sesame oil**
- ❖ **2 tbsp. cornstarch**
- ❖ **2 tbsp. water**

**Minutes**

:05   Heat up the 1 cup of water to boiling. While waiting, rinse chicken breasts and remove skins.

:05   Place the chicken bouillon cube in mixing bowl and add the 1 cup of boiling water. Fully dissolve the cube to make chicken broth.

:10   Rinse celery and green onions. Chop all into bite size pieces. Add to crock pot. Also mix in ground ginger.

4:30   In a small bowl, combine the chicken broth with soy sauce. Pour mixture over chicken. Cover and cook on LOW for 4 hours and 30 minutes.

:10   After cooking on LOW, prepare cooking of brown rice by boiling amount of water as needed.

:10   Add rice to water boiling and simmer covered for 45 minutes (or time designated).

:10   Rinse off mushrooms and bean sprouts. Slice mushrooms.

:05   Turn control to HIGH. Add mushroom slices and bean sprouts. Cover and cook on HIGH 5 minutes.

:05   Drizzle oil over food in crock pot. Stir to mix. Dissolve cornstarch in 2 tbsp. water and stir into chicken mixture in crock pot.

:10   Cover and cook on HIGH 15 minutes. Rinse off broccoli and chop up for cooking.

:02   Use a large frying pan to stir-fry the broccoli. Preheat 2 minutes at high heat with about 2 tbsp. of water.

:03   Toss in broccoli pieces and cover pan. Check after 3 minutes to make sure there still is water left. If needed, added another 2 tbsp. of water.

:05   Crock pot dinner is now complete. Turn off and set aside for serving! Remove rice from heat and let sit for 5 minutes. Broccoli is now ready and dinner is complete!

# Chicken & Mushrooms
# in a Dry Cooker with Chinese Style Vegetables

**Great tastes involved with a variety of seasonings - onions, garlic and soy sauce - make this another light and nutritious dinner.**
**Total completion time: 56 minutes**

- ❖ **4 chicken breasts**
- ❖ **2½ cups water**
- ❖ **6 green onions**
- ❖ **1 cup Mahatma brown rice**
- ❖ **2 large celery sticks**
- ❖ **½ white onion**
- ❖ **8 oz. canned chopped mushrooms**
- ❖ **slab of salted butter**
- ❖ **1 tbsp. olive oil**
- ❖ **½ tsp. Lawry's garlic powder**

- ❖ **1 dash of salt & pepper**
- ❖ **1 green bell pepper**
- ❖ **1 pinch of salt**
- ❖ **1 pinch of pepper**
- ❖ **½ cube of salted butter**
- ❖ **½ cup whole milk**
- ❖ **4 oz. jack cheese**
- ❖ **1 tbsp. KIKKOMAM® Soy Sauce**
- ❖ **¼ cup sliced almonds**

**Minutes**

**:05** Rinse off chicken and remove skins. De-bone chicken breasts by cutting lengthwise up against bone. Keep chicken slabs no fatter than ¾ inch thick.

**:05** Preheat 2 ½ cups of water in small pot needed for cooking of brown rice.

**:02** Water for rice should now be boiling. Add rice and set up timer.

**:05** Rinse and chop green onions.

**:03** Rub chicken slabs with oil and then sprinkle with garlic powder, and dash of salt and pepper.

**:03** Oil dry cooker with butter and heat with lid on over medium flame 2 to 3 minutes.

**:03** Add chicken and cook at high heat 3 minutes with cover on.

**:15** Adjust dry cooker to low heat and cook 20 minutes, shaking occasionally. In a separate pan, fully melt butter, milk, and cheese - stirring together. Set aside. Use this time now to prepare the Chinese style vegetables. Rinse off all vegetables. Finely shred the green cabbage, diagonally slice celery sticks, chop onion, and cut bell pepper into thin slices.

**:05** Heat a large frying pan with 2 tbsp. of water to boiling. Add the cut vegetables and cover the pan. Maintain at high heat for 5 to 7 minutes. After the first 3 minutes double check that water has not fully evaporated. If needed, add another 2 tbsp. of water.

**:02** Add mushrooms and green onions to cheese sauce and mix in.
Pour sauce over chicken. Cover pan and cook 10 more minutes over low heat.

**:08** Vegetables are now done. Season with a dash of salt and pepper.
Check on rice and remove when done. Remove chicken from heat and garnish with almonds. Dinner is now complete!

# Chicken Noodle Dinner

Once again, multiple vegetables included in my single dish oven casserole engage a colorful and appealing presentation to be delivered to you - meat, vegetables, and carbs all in one package!  Total completion time: 50 minutes

- ❖ **½ cup milk**
- ❖ **3 tablespoons of salted butter**
- ❖ **1¼ cups water**
- ❖ **1 box of Fettuccine Alfredo pasta & sauce (4.5 - 5.5 oz.)**
- ❖ **2 carrots**
- ❖ **2 oz. sliced almonds**

- ❖ **1 green bell pepper**
- ❖ **1 red bell pepper**
- ❖ **2 celery sticks**
- ❖ **2 cooked chicken breasts (this is when you can refer to my tips on pre-cooking chicken)**

- ❖ **A simple salad accompanies well.**

**Minutes**

:05   In a medium saucepan, combine milk, butter, and water - as well as the pasta and any seasonings enclosed in the fettuccine alfredo box.  I now go with the measurements that I use for a box that is 4.7 oz. in size.  Make sure to check the measurements that they ask for in the pasta you are using regarding milk, butter, and water - and use them accordingly.  Go by the time slot they allow for the preparation of their product as well as any directions they may have that varies from mine.  Bring to a boil and cook as they direct. This whole process will take about 10 to 14 minutes, allowing for the cooking.

:05   Rinse off all vegetables and proceed to chop into bite-size pieces.

:05   Check the noodles. When done, let the pot sit over no flame, allowing the sauce to thicken.

:05   Chop the chicken breasts into bite-size pieces.

:05   Preheat oven to 350°.
In a large bowl, stir the chicken and vegetables into the prepared noodles. Place in a 3-quart oven dish.

:25   Bake, uncovered for 25 minutes. Use this time to prepare a simple salad.
Pull dish out of oven. Before serving your meal, stir and garnish with the almonds.  Enjoy!

# Chicken in Mellow White Cream Sauce

This stove-top dinner can be arranged anytime at the drop of a dime. It's easy to keep all recipe ingredients in stock in the kitchen and freezer. Use a cellophane bag to store pre-cooked chicken.

Total completion time: 50 minutes

- ❖ **3 medium chicken breasts – pre-cooked**
- ❖ **1 small white onion**
- ❖ **2 tbsp. olive oil**
- ❖ **½ cup white wine**
- ❖ **½ cup chicken broth (see Tip)**
- ❖ **1 tbsp. tarragon**
- ❖ **al dente® All-Natural Carba-Nada Egg Fettuccini Noodles**

- ❖ **Salad**

- ❖ **2/3 cup heavy cream**
- ❖ **16 oz. frozen green beans**
- ❖ **1 pinch black pepper**
- ❖ **1 tbsp. parsley flakes**

- ❖ **Kraft ® grated parmesan for flavoring of each individual plate**

**Minutes**

- :15   Make a salad ahead of time and set in refrigerator, covered with clear cellophane - holes punched in.
- :10   Chop chicken breasts into 1 inch chunks.
- :04   Mince onion.
- :01   Pre-heat a large frying pan 1 minute.
- :02   Add olive oil. Spread around and add onion. Stir-fry at medium heat for 2 minutes.
- :06   Add wine, broth, and tarragon. Bring to a boil, then simmer 3 minutes, stirring occasionally.
- :02   For the pasta, fill up a pot 2/3 full with water. Bring to a boil.
- :03   To the frying pan, stir in cream, chicken, green beans, pepper, and parsley. Heat up over medium heat. When done, remove pot from heat and allow sauce to thicken.
- :05   Add pasta to the pot of water. Set timer for pasta (generally 5 minutes).
- :02   Check that pasta. Done!

**Tip** If you do not have the broth at your disposal, boil 1 cup of water, add 1 chicken bouillon cube and stir. This will give you the needed broth (just use the ½ cup needed).

# Chicken Tetrazzini in a Crock Pot

This is one crock pot meal that ranks top-notch with my family – very delicious. One advantage of this feast is that you can pre-cook the breasts ahead of time and store them in the refrigerator or freezer. Otherwise, allow about 20 minutes in the morning to pre-cook the chicken breasts in a large pot of water.  Cook in the crock pot 1 hour on high and 6 to 7 hours on low. Total completion time: 8 hours

- **2 large breasts - pre-cooked**
- **½ tsp. salt**
- **8 oz. sliced mushrooms, liquid removed**
- **2 cups chicken broth (see Tip)**
- **¼ cup milk**
- **10 oz. Campbell's® Cream of Mushroom Soup**
- **4 oz. sliced almonds**

- **1 small onion**
- **1 broccoli crown**
- **8 oz. al dente® All-Natural Carba-Nada Egg Fettuccini Noodles**
- **Kraft ® grated parmesan for flavoring of each individual plate**

## Minutes

**:05**  Fill a large pot with water and heat to boiling. Rinse the chicken breasts and remove skins. Halfway along the side of the meat, fully slice into the meat to lessen the thickness for easier and faster cooking.

**:20**  Place chicken in pot of water and bring back to full boil. Add ½ tsp. salt.

**:05**  Remove chicken from heat. At this point you can save the broth from the pot.
Pour liquid through the strainer, filtering out any chicken residue. Set aside 2 cups of it.

**:30**  Using a sharp knife, strip chicken off the bones and dice.

**1:00**  Place chicken, mushrooms, broth, milk, cream of mushroom soup, and almonds in crock pot. Stir together. Cook on high 1 hour.

**5:45**  Set crock pot on low.

**:05**  Cut the onion into wedges and add to the crock pot.

**:01**  Prepare a pot for the cooking of your pasta. Bring water to a boil.
Rinse off the broccoli and chop.

**:04**  Heat up a frying pan with 2 tbsp. of water and add  broccoli. Cover up and cook for 5 minutes at high heat. Add a bit more water if needed, but make sure it doesn't fully evaporate.

**:01**  Add pasta to water and bring back to boil. Set timer for 5 minutes or whatever pasta instructions designate.

**:04**  Broccoli is now done.
Pasta should now be done. Dinner is ready!  Serve with grated parmesan cheese.

*Tip*  If you choose to do this recipe with prior cooked chicken and do not have the broth at your disposal, boil 2 cups of water, add 2 chicken bouillon cubes and stir.  This will give you the needed broth.

# Coq au Vin in a Crock Pot

**This is a delicious, light, and tasty dinner that works very well as a simple meal to be prepared ahead of time. One thing possible is to fully prepare this in a crock pot and store it in a refrigerator 24 hours ahead of time. Just allow an extra half-hour cooking on LOW to make up for the cold temperature of the pot. Total completion time: 8 hours and 25 minutes**

- *1 cup water*
- *1 Herb ox® chicken bouillon cube*
- *3 chicken breasts or dark meat (2½ to 3 lbs.)*
- *4 green onions (½ cup)*
- *½ lb. whole mushrooms*
- *1 cup red wine*
- *¼ tsp. Lawry's® garlic powder*
- *1 pinch salt*
- *1 tbsp. parsley flakes*
- *½ tsp. dried thyme leaves*
- *¼ tsp. black pepper*
- *8 boiling onions*
- *6 small potatoes*
- *1 bay leaf*
- *1 broccoli crown*

## Minutes

**:05**   Heat 1 cup of water to boiling for making of chicken broth.

**:05**   Mix bouillon cube in water to make the chicken broth. Remove skins from chicken. Rinse off and place in crock pot. Pour broth over chicken.

**:05**   Rinse green onions and chop. Put in crock pot. Add mushrooms.

**:05**   Pour red wine in. Sprinkle in garlic powder, salt, parsley, thyme leaves, and black pepper. Put in the boiling onions.

**7:50**   Scrub potatoes clean and add to food. Top with the bay leaf and close the crock pot. Set the temperature on low. This will be cooking for 7 to 8 hours.

**:05**   Rinse off the broccoli. Proceed to chop into medium or small pieces.

**:03**   Preheat a large frying pan with 2 tbsp. of water.

**:07**   Toss in the broccoli pieces. Maintaining flame or heat, cover the pan and cook. If water evaporates and you do not wish broccoli to char, add another 2 tbsp. of water. Otherwise, enjoy the burnt taste.   Broccoli is now done and dinner is complete!

# *Curry Chicken*

Here I give you a simple taste of the curry chicken that introduced me to Asian food. It's a healthy, light, and easy stove-top dinner to cook. Total completion time: 45 minutes

- ❖ *1 medium onion*
- ❖ *1 green bell pepper*
- ❖ *2 celery sticks*
- ❖ *2 cups pre-cooked chicken*
- ❖ *1 red apple*
- ❖ *2¼ cups water*

- ❖ *1 cup Uncle Ben's® white rice*
- ❖ *2 cups water*
- ❖ *2 chicken bouillon cubes*
- ❖ *¼ cup salted butter*

- ❖ *1 tsp. curry powder*
- ❖ *1 pinch salt*
- ❖ *¼ cup white flour*
- ❖ *1 broccoli crown*
- ❖ *peanuts*

**Minutes**

:03   Chop onion, bell pepper, and celery. Thinly slice the apple.

:05   Heat 2 cups of water to boiling.

:02   Mix bouillon cubes into the 2 cups of boiling water to make chicken broth.

:02   Melt butter in large saucepan. Add onion, bell pepper, and celery. Cook over low heat. Stir in curry powder, salt, and flour, mixing until hot.

:06   Start 2 ¼ cups of water boiling in a small pot in which to cook the rice.

:01   Cut up cooked chicken into small cubed pieces.

:05   Add rice to the small pot of boiling water. Cover and simmer for 20 minutes, or whatever time is specified for cooking the rice.

:06   Pour chicken broth into saucepan and stir constantly at high heat until mixture reaches a boil. Stir and boil one minute more.

:01   Stir meat in; heat through while occasionally stirring for about 12 more minutes.

:04   Rinse off broccoli and cut to bite-size pieces.

:03   Heat 2 tbsp. of water in large frying pan to boiling.

:01   Add broccoli pieces to frying pan. Cook on high heat, covered, for 5 minutes. Add more water if necessary - don't allow pan to get dry. .

:04   Rice is done; remove from heat and set for 5 minutes to cool before serving.

:02   Broccoli is to be removed from heat. Add the apple slices to the chicken.
        Dinner is now done. Serve the curry chicken over rice and top with peanuts.

*Tip* * You may use 3 chicken breasts, 4 chicken thighs, or 7 legs. Chicken can be pre-cooked in a pot of boiling water. Slice thick breasts or thighs lengthwise to equate time needed for cooking chicken pieces. Keep fully doused in water, maintaining a   boiling state. Cook for 15 minutes. See that the meat easily separates showing it is fully cooked - no red meat. Broth can be used for recipe. Just remove the top layer of fat.

# *Crunched Chicken Strips*

This very tasty dinner is quite simple to cook and is very popular. By using cornflake cereal bits, you achieve crunchy texture on the chicken meat without needless calories or the fat content of deep frying. The chicken needs to be marinated in Italian salad dressing ahead of time. You can either marinate chicken strips in the refrigerator the night before, or as late as one hour before putting them in the oven. I'm introducing the recipe to you as if you were starting the same afternoon, with only an hour for marinating. Total completion time: 2 hours

- ❖ *4 chicken breasts*
- ❖ *1 cup Newman's Own® Italian salad dressing*
- ❖ *1 large onion*
- ❖ *2 cups of Kellogg's Cornflakes® Cereal*
- ❖ *1 broccoli crown*

- ❖ *4 large potatoes*
- ❖ *Salt*
- ❖ *¼ cup of salted butter (½ cube)*
- ❖ *2 tblsp. of half-and-half cream*

**Minutes**

:15    Remove skins off the chicken breasts, then proceed to remove chicken from bones. Cut into strips about 1 to1½ inches wide and 3 to 4 inches long.

:05    Place all strips flat in a container. Fill with Italian salad dressing so all chicken is covered. Cover container and place in refrigerator for an hour.

:05    Thinly slice the onion for the chicken and set aside.

:35    Place the cereal flakes in a cellophane sealed bag and proceed to pound the flakes until finely crunched.

:07    Use this time now to start those smashed potatoes. Fill a pot halfway with water and heat up to boiling.

:03    Rinse off the potatoes. Then, using a cutting board as your base, peel the potatoes. Cut up into 8 pieces or so per potato - making the potato pieces small in size so they cook faster.

:02    Place foil on a cookie sheet. Spread onion slices on the foil. Preheat oven to 350°.

:03    Place the potato pieces into the pot of water. Add about 3 sprinkles of salt. If the water has not yet gotten to boiling, it's alright, just keep the heat on high flame. Simply make sure the potatoes stay fully covered with water while cooking. Allow about ½ an inch from the water to the top of the pan - so there is room for boiling water and it does not overflow onto the stove. When the water is at a full boil, lower the flame a bit while maintaining the boil.

:10    Remove the chicken strips from the refrigerator and place in the cellophane bag. Shake to fully cover each piece with the flakes.

:05    Place chicken strips on the onion slices.

**Minutes**

**:10**    Place cookie sheet in oven for 30 minutes.

Start checking the potatoes by poking with a fork. When the potatoes are quite soft and poke easily, turn off the flame. Drain water out of the pot. Slice the butter into thin slabs and add to the potatoes all over while mixing in with a fork.

**:05**    Add half and half cream to the potatoes gradually while mixing in. Now use a stainless steel utensil as a potato masher to smash your potatoes. Let this be your opportunity for the day to take out any aggressions or upsets on your potatoes!!! Give yourself a little taste to make sure they are buttery enough for you.

**:05**    Rinse off the broccoli and cut into bite-size pieces.

**:02**    Preheat a frying pan and pour in 2 tbsp. of water. Bring to a boil.

**:03**    Add the broccoli pieces and cover the pan, maintaining high heat.

**:02**    Check broccoli. If needed, add another 2 tbsp. of water. Do not allow all water to evaporate.

**:03**    Broccoli is now ready. Turn off and remove any water.

Your dinner is now done!

# Dry Cooker Chicken Strips with Vegetable Stir-Fry

This dry cooker dinner enables you to slice or chop vegetables as the chicken cooks. Using the dry cooker I mentioned earlier in the book allows you to char the meat, as well as cook it fast with much flavor. This technique also provides much flavor for cooking the green bell pepper, celery, and onion wedges that accompany the chicken dish. Serving this meal with teriyaki sauce is a very good balance with the seasoning on the vegetables. Brown rice works well for accompaniment.  The Vegetable Stir-Fry is to be cooked in a large frying pan.  Total completion time: 55 minutes

## Ingredients for rice

- ❖ 2½ cups water
- ❖ 1 cup Mahatma® brown rice

## Ingredients for dry cooker chicken strips

- ❖ 3 chicken breasts
- ❖ 1 slab of salted butter
- ❖ ¼ tsp. pepper
- ❖ ¼ tsp. Lawry's® garlic powder
- ❖ light sprinkle of salt
- ❖ 1 small onion
- ❖ 1 green bell pepper
- ❖ 2 celery stalks
- ❖ teriyaki sauce

## Ingredients for vegetable stir-fry

- ❖ 6 large mushrooms
- ❖ 1 tbsp. sesame seeds
- ❖ 1 tsp. sesame oil
- ❖ 1 tbsp. olive oil
- ❖ ½ tsp. Lawry's® garlic powder
- ❖ 1 tbsp. sweet chili sauce
- ❖ 1 tsp. ginger powder
- ❖ 1 tbsp. KIKKOMAN® Soy  Sauce
- ❖ 2 green onions
- ❖ 1 broccoli crown
- ❖ 1 red bell pepper
- ❖ 1 yellow bell pepper
- ❖ 1 tbsp. Bradshaw's Spun® Premium Honey
- ❖ ¼ cup black olives, liquid drained
- ❖ 1 green bell pepper

**Minutes**

:05    Set up 2 ½ cups of water to cook brown rice in and bring to a boil.

:05    Cook rice.

:10    Because the vegetable stir-fry dish involves many vegetables, I always cut them ahead of time and set them aside to cook later in a large frying pan. Rinse the vegetables first, and then proceed to slice up the green onions, cut up broccoli into bite size pieces, slice the red, yellow, and green bell peppers into strips about 1 inch thick, and thinly slice the mushrooms. Set aside.

:07    Rinse the chicken breasts and remove any skin or fat. Cut into strips about 1-inch thick. Season chicken strips with pepper and garlic, and a light sprinkle of salt.

:03    Fully oil the dry cooker with 1 slab of butter. Heat with a lid on for 2 to 3 minutes.

:10    Place chicken strips in dry cooker and cover with lid. Put on medium/high heat and cook about 10 minutes, with alternative shaking of pan, about every 3 minutes, until chicken is browned. Rinse off vegetables to be cooked with the chicken (green bell pepper and celery). Proceed to thinly slice green bell pepper and chop celery into 1 inch pieces. Cut onion into wedges. Remember to shake dry cooker pan a few times while the chicken is cooking.

:01    Remove chicken, set aside, and re-oil dry cooker lightly with butter. Add green bell pepper, celery, and onion wedges. Stir fry 5 to 7 minutes.

:02    Place sesame seeds on a small sheet of foil to be toasted in toaster oven - 2 minutes or until golden. Set aside.

:02    Heat both oils in a large pan. Add garlic, ginger, and green onion pieces. Stir-fry 1 minute over medium heat.

:02    Add broccoli, red, yellow, and green pepper slices, mushroom slices, and olives. Stir-fry 2 minutes. Combine soy sauce, honey, and chili sauce. Mix well.

:03    Remove vegetable pan from heat. Pour mixed soy sauce over vegetables and toss lightly to mix. Sprinkle with sesame seeds.

:05    Return chicken back to dry cooker pan and re-warm. Rice is done. Remove from heat and let cool for 5 minutes.

       Dinner is now ready! Serve with that teriyaki sauce!

# Garam Masala Chicken with Cheddar Garden Pasta

**Garam Masala Indian Seasoning powder with olive oil gives a unique flavoring to this simple chicken recipe. My Cheddar Garden Pasta recipe accompanies the dinner well, bringing in carrots as your vegetable content. My daughter tagged it *Aka - best pasta ever!* Total completion time: 1 hour**

## Ingredients for Garam Masala chicken

- **4 chicken breasts**
- **2 tbsp. Garam Masala® Indian Seasoning powder**
- **4 tbsp. water**
- **4 tbsp. olive oil**

## Ingredients for cheddar garden pasta

- **4 oz. cheddar cheese**
- **2 oz. jack cheese**
- **6 carrots**
- **½ of a 12 oz. Anthony's egg noodles package**
- **½ tsp. dried basil**
- **10¾ oz. Campbell's® Cream of Celery Soup**
- **1 tbsp. salted butter**
- **1/3 cup milk**

**Minutes**

:10 Rinse chicken breasts, removing skin and excess fat.
De-bone chicken breasts - cutting alongside the bone. Keep the chicken slices no fatter than about 1 inch in thickness.

:05 Mix seasoning, oil, and 4 tbsp. water in a plastic bag that can be sealed.
Add chicken pieces and shake to fully coat.

:03 Let chicken marinate in seasoning for 15 minutes.

:04 Shred cheeses and set aside.

:03 Peel carrots. Slice in half and then lengthwise by fourths.

:05 Preheat oven to 350°. Cover a cookie sheet with foil.

:06 Place chicken on foil and in oven for 30 minutes.

:04 Heat a pot of water to cook pasta in.

:08 Add pasta to boiling water and cook 8 minutes.

:01 Pasta is now ready. Drain out water.

:01 Preheat a large frying pan with ¼ cup of water.

:03 Add carrot slices and cook over medium flame with cover on for 3 minutes.

:01 In a large pot melt butter over low flame, and add basil - stirring for 1 minute.

:06 Stir in soup, milk, and cheeses, and heat until cheese melts.  Add carrots and pasta.
Toss together. Pull chicken out of oven because dinner is now ready!

# *Italianized Chicken with a Spicy Kick in a Crock Pot*

**This flavorful recipe gives you the gift of peace and time to do lots of other things because it cooks in the crock pot. Prep time for the main dish itself is only about 15 minutes! The broccoli will only take you 10 minutes to clean and cook, and the low-carb pasta will cook in about 5 minutes! Go for it!! Total completion time: 10 hours**

- ❖ *1 medium-sized onion*
- ❖ *4 chicken breasts*
- ❖ *14½ oz. can Italian stewed tomatoes*
- ❖ *1 tbsp. capers*
- ❖ *¼ tsp. black pepper*
- ❖ *½ tsp. Lawry's® garlic powder*
- ❖ *4 oz. Manzanilla® whole green olives*

- ❖ *4 oz. black olives*
- ❖ *al dente® All-Natural Carba-Nada Egg Fettucine Noodles*
- ❖ *1 broccoli crown*

- ❖ *Kraft ® grated parmesan for flavoring of each individual plate*

**Minutes**

- **:15**    Slice the onion and separate slices.
Rinse off chicken breasts and remove skins.
- **:05**    Place chicken breasts in crock pot. Lay onion slices on top. Stir tomatoes with capers, pepper, and garlic, and pour mixture on top (including the liquid from the tomatoes can). Add olives on top (without liquid from the can of olives). Cook on low.
- **9:25**    Let's say you're aiming the dinner for 6:00...At this time you'll want to work on the remainder of the meal.
- **:05**    Start a pot of water heating to a boil for the low-carb pasta to be cooked.
Rinse and cut the broccoli.
- **:01**    Place the pasta in the pot. Set timer.
- **:02**    Heat up a large frying pan for 2 minutes with a 2 tbsp. of water.
- **:05**    Toss the broccoli pieces in. Cover and cook for 5 minutes at high heat. Make sure water does not fully evaporate. If necessary, add a bit more water.
- **:02**    Broccoli is now done. Remove from heat.
The chicken dinner is now also complete. Reactionary taste buds ahead!

*Tip* * Instead of using full chicken breasts, you may want to slice the chicken into strips about 3" long by 1" wide. After rinsing off the chicken breasts in the first step above, allow 10 minutes for slicing the chicken into strips. In the step above, where it states 9:25 for crock pot time, cutting the chicken into strips will shorten cook time to 5 – 6 hours. The overall time for this recipe would then be 5¾ to 6 ¾ hours.

# Intoxicated Chicken

**I have never known a taste bud to reject this meal. The chicken is light, tasty, and mellow.  Smashed potatoes and broccoli accompany this one beautifully. Total completion time: 1 hour and 25 minutes**

- ❖ **4 chicken breasts**
- ❖ **¾ cup white wine**
- ❖ **1 medium sized onion**
- ❖ **1 pinch black pepper**

- ❖ **½ teaspoon Lawry's® garlic powder**
- ❖ **1 teaspoon paprika**
- ❖ **4 large potatoes**

- ❖ **¼ cup of salted butter (½ cube)**
- ❖ **2 tbsp. of half-and- half cream**
- ❖ **1 broccoli crown**

## Minutes

:05  Clean chicken breasts, rinsing them off with water.  Remove chicken skins with a paring knife and remove any excess fat.

:05  Preheat oven to 375°.

:10  Place the breasts in an oven-proof dish – 3-quart size. Pour wine over the chicken. Slice off top and bottom sections of the onion, and remove outside skin. Then cut up in slices and proceed to chop up.

:05  Season breasts with sprinkles of pepper and paprika, and then garlic powder. Spread onion pieces across chicken breasts.

:20  Cover dish and place in oven for 1 hour.
While the chicken is cooking in the oven, I use this time to prepare smashed potatoes and broccoli.

:05  Fill a pot halfway up with water and heat to boiling.
Rinse off the potatoes. Then, using a cutting board as your base, peel the potatoes. Cut up into 8 pieces or so per potato - making the potato pieces small in size so they cook faster.

:15  Place the potato pieces into the pot of water. Add about 3 sprinkles of salt. If the water has boil, it's alright, just keep the heat on high flame. Simply make sure the potatoes stay fully covered with water while cooking. Allow about ½ an inch from the water to the top of the pan - so there is room for boiling water and it does not overflow onto the stove. When the water is at a full boil, lower the flame a bit while maintaining the boil.

:05  Start checking the potatoes by poking with a fork. When the potatoes are quite soft and poke easily, turn off the flame. Drain water out of the pot. Slice the butter into thin slabs and add to the potatoes all over while mixing in with a fork.

:05  Rinse off broccoli and cut to bite-size pieces.

:02  Add half and half cream to the potatoes gradually while mixing in. Now use a stainless steel utensil/potato masher to smash potatoes.  (Let this be your opportunity for the day to take out any aggressions or upsets on the potatoes!!!)  Give yourself a little taste to make sure they are buttery enough for you. If desired, add a bit more butter!
Put a cover on the potatoes/pan to keep warm.

**Minutes**

:03    Heat 2 tbsp. of water in large frying pan to boiling.

:05    Add broccoli pieces. Cook on high heat, covered, for 5 minutes.  Add more water if necessary - don't allow pan to get dry.

Chicken is now to be removed from the oven.  All dinner is ready for serving!

# *Smashed Potato Chicken Bowl*

**This is a savory dinner that appeals to all and gives you lots of nutrition, with all of the necessary food groups in one dish!  Total completion time: 2 hours**

## Ingredients for chicken filling

- *3 medium pre-cooked chicken breasts (if not pre-cooked – start when instructed below)*

## Ingredients for smashed potato bowl

- *pat of salted butter*
- *10 oz. mixed vegetables*
- *10 ¾ oz. Campbell's® Cream of Chicken Soup*
- *¼ cup of milk*
- *1 pinch black pepper*
- *½ tsp. ground mustard*
- *½ tsp. Lawry's® garlic powder*
- *4 large potatoes*

- *Salad*

- *1 pinch salt*
- *8 oz. jack cheese*
- *½ cube of salted butter*
- *2 tblsp. of half-and-half cream*
- *6 oz. (¾ cup) of canned Durkee's® French Fried Onions (divided: ¼ cup and ½ cup)*

## Minutes

**:20**  If you do not have pre-cooked chicken for the recipe - start now. Fill a medium-size pot with water and bring to a boil. Rinse off your chicken breasts, remove any skin, and slice into strips for faster cooking. Put the strips into the pot of water, even if not boiling yet. Use this time to shred that jack cheese! Set aside for later.

**:05**  Your chicken should be done at this point. Remove from hot water.

**:10**  Fill a pot halfway up with water and heat to boiling. Rinse the potatoes. Then, using a cutting board as your base, peel the potatoes. Cut into 8 pieces or so per potato - making the potato pieces small in size so they cook faster.

**:02**  Place the potato pieces into the pot of water. Add a few sprinkles of salt. If the water is not yet boiling, it's alright, just keep the heat on high flame. Simply make sure the potatoes stay fully covered with water while cooking. Allow about ½ an inch from the water to top of the pan so there is room for boiling water and it does not overflow onto the stove. When the water comes to a full boil, lower the flame a bit while maintaining the boil.

**Minutes**

**:08**  Now take the pre-cooked chicken and cut into cubes. It should equal about 2 cups. Set aside.

**:05**  Start checking the potatoes by poking with a fork. When the potatoes are quite soft and poke easily, turn off the flame. Drain water out of the pot. Slice the butter into thin slabs and add to the potatoes all over while mixing in with a fork.

**:07**  Add half and half cream to the potatoes gradually while mixing in. Now use a stainless steel utensil/potato masher to smash your potatoes. Let this be your opportunity for the day to take out any aggressions or upsets on your potatoes!!! Smash into a smooth and even texture. Give yourself a little taste to make sure they are buttery enough for you.

**:05**  In the pot mix into the potatoes ½ cup of the cheese and ½ the can of the crispy onions. Using a bit of soft butter, grease a 2-quart casserole dish. Preheat oven to 375º.

**:04**  Now spread the potato mixture into the casserole dish on the bottom and on the sides to make a bowl.

**:04**  Aside, mix the chicken, vegetables, soup, ¼ cup of milk, pepper, ground mustard, and garlic powder. Pour into the potato bowl.

**:40**  Place in the oven and bake, uncovered, for 40 minutes.
Prep salad.

**:05**  Remove from oven to top with remaining cheese and crispy onions. Return to oven for 5 minutes.

**:05**  Remove from oven and let stand for 5 minutes before serving.
Dinner is now ready for you to eat!

# Lemon Honey Chicken

**Lemon tartness is reduced with honey and olive oil, and a great mellow taste is acquired as a result.  Total completion time: 3 hours and 5 minutes**

**I have found that half an hour preparation for this meal is enough. Time is needed for the chicken to marinate - 20 minutes to 2 hours. Baking time is 40 minutes.**

- ❖ *4 chicken breasts*
- ❖ *2 lemons*
- ❖ *1½ tbsp. Bradshaw's Spun® Premium Honey*
- ❖ *2¼ tbsp. olive oil*
- ❖ *1 broccoli crown*

- ❖ *1 pinch salt*
- ❖ *1 pinch black pepper*
- ❖ *2½ cups water*
- ❖ *1 cup Mahatma® brown rice*

**Minutes**

| | |
|---|---|
| **:20** | Remove skins and wash the chicken breasts. On a cutting board, using a sharp paring knife, separate chicken meat from bones, leaving them fully de-boned. |
| **:05** | Rinse the lemon and strain out the juice. Set aside 6 tablespoons. Grate 2 tsp. worth of lemon peel.  Mix lemon juice, honey, oil, salt, pepper, and lemon peel. |
| **1:50** | Place chicken in large baking dish. Cover chicken with mixture, turning over to fully coat. Cover dish and place in refrigerator to marinate for the 2 hours. |
| **:05** | In medium pot, heat 2½ cups of water to boiling. |
| **:05** | Add the 1 cup brown rice and stir in. Put on simmer and set timer to 45 minutes.  Preheat oven to 375º. |
| **:30** | Place chicken dish in oven and set timer for 40 minutes. |
| **:04** | Rinse off broccoli and cut to bite-size pieces. |
| **:01** | Heat 2 tbsp. of water in large frying pan to boiling. |
| **:05** | Add broccoli pieces. Cook on high heat, covered, for 5 minutes. Add more water if necessary - don't allow pan to get dry.  Although the steps since placing the chicken in the refrigerator took only 50 minutes, here you will just wait the remaining 1 hour and 10 minutes before removing it. |
| | Dinner is now ready! |

# Orange Bunny Chicken

**This great colorful chicken dinner with carrots is for someone with a sweet tooth and it can be prepped bunny-hopping fast before placing in the oven. Total completion time: 1 hour and 20 minutes**

- **4 chicken breasts**
- **4 large carrots**
- **6 oz. orange juice concentrate – defrosted**
- **2 tbsp. cornstarch**
- **dash of salt**
- **1 pinch of black pepper**

- **6 green onions**
- **lettuce for salad**
- **2 celery sticks**
- **4 radishes**
- **Anthony's® egg noodles**

- **Kraft ® grated parmesan for flavoring of each individual plate**

**Minutes**

**:05** Preheat oven 375º. Remove chicken skins and rinse chicken. Place chicken pieces in a baking dish.

**:05** Peel carrots, chop off ends, then cut in half. Slice each section lengthwise four times to make slim slices.

**:05** Distribute carrot slices atop chicken pieces.

**:05** In bowl mix orange juice concentrate, cornstarch, salt, and pepper. Pour over chicken and carrots.

**:05** Cover dish with foil or glass cover and bake in oven 45 minutes.

**:05** Remove tips off green onions and proceed to chop. Set aside for later.

**:20** Wash and tear lettuce, chop celery, and slice radishes. This will simply make a quick salad to accompany dinner.

**:10** Start water boiling in pot for cooking of pasta.

**:05** Place noodles in pot of boiling water - these noodles generally take 8-11 minutes, but remember...water has to return to a full boil with the noodles in it before you start timing it.

**:05** Pull dish out of oven. Baste chicken with juices and distribute onion pieces on top. Cover dish again and return to oven 10 more minutes.

**:05** Check noodles to see if they are ready yet. If so, remove from heat, drain water, and set aside covered to keep warm.

**:05** Remove chicken from oven.
Enjoy your orange bunny chicken dinner now escorted by that salad!

# Oriental Chicken & Grapes with Chinese Style Vegetables

Flavoring of mustard, soy sauce, spun honey, and garlic powder give a wonderful spunk to the chicken breasts when you sprinkle them with sesame seeds and add grapes. This entree is marvelously complimented by brown rice and the Chinese Style Vegetable I gave you to accompany the Dry Cooker Chicken & Mushroom Dinner.

**Total completion time: 1 hour and 10 minutes**

* *4 chicken breasts*
* *2½ cups water for rice*
* *2 cups seedless grapes*
* *½ head of small green cabbage*
* *2 large celery sticks*
* *½ white onion*
* *1 green bell pepper*
* *1 cup Mahatma® brown rice*
* *3 tbsp. mustard*
* *3 tbsp. KIKKOMAN® Soy Sauce*
* *2 tbsp. Bradshaw's Spun® Honey*
* *¼ tsp. Lawry's® garlic powder*
* *2 tbsp. sesame seeds*
* *1 pinch salt*
* *1 pinch black pepper*
* *1 tbsp. KIKKOMAN® Soy Sauce*

**Minutes**

:10   Preheat oven to 400º and proceed to clean chicken breasts. Rinse them off with water; remove chicken skins with a paring knife, and remove any excess fat. Rinse off grapes and all vegetables.

:05   Preheat water in pot needed for cooking of brown rice. Use this time now to prepare vegetables for cooking. Finely shred the cabbage, thinly slice celery sticks, chop onion, and cut bell pepper into thin diagonal slices. Set aside.

:05   Place the chicken in an oven-proof dish – 3-quart size - and cover. Bake in oven for 20 minutes.

:05   Water for rice should now be boiling. Add rice, lower flame to simmer, and set up timer (brown rice generally takes 45 minutes).

:10   Mix mustard, 3 tbsp. soy sauce, spun honey, and garlic powder.

:05   Remove chicken from oven and drain out fat. Brush both sides of chicken breasts with the mustard mixture. Freely sprinkle sesame seeds on the chicken.

:20   Place chicken back in oven and set for another 25 minutes.

:05   Heat a large frying pan with ½ cup of water at high heat in which to cook vegetables. Add the vegetables and cover the pan. Maintain at high heat for 5-7 minutes. After the first 3 minutes, double check that water has not fully evaporated. If needed, add another ½ cup of water.

:05   Pull chicken out of oven, baste, and add the grapes. Set in oven for 5 more minutes. Check on rice. Remove from heat when done. Vegetables are now ready. Sprinkle with salt and pepper, and mix in 1 tbsp. soy sauce.
Ready now!

# *Quick Italian Chicken*

**Lots of cheeeeeese adorns the spiced-up chicken with great texture and taste.
Total completion time: 55 minutes**

- ❖ **2½ cups water**
- ❖ **1 cup Mahatma® brown rice**
- ❖ **1 lb. green beans**
- ❖ **4 chicken breasts**
- ❖ **8 oz. jack cheese**
- ❖ **2 cans (14½ oz. ea.) stewed Italian tomatoes**

- ❖ **2 tbsp. cornstarch**
- ❖ **½ tsp. oregano**
- ❖ **½ tsp. basil**
- ❖ **2/3 cup grated Kraft® parmesan cheese**
- ❖ **1 tbsp. parsley flakes**

**Minutes**

- **:05** Heat 2½ cups of water to boiling.
- **:05** Put 1 cup rice in boiling water. Place stovetop burner on simmer and set timer for 45 minutes.
- **:05** Rinse the green beans and chop off ends. Set aside.
- **:05** Preheat oven to 425°.
- **:05** Place the chicken breasts on a cutting board and remove meat from the bones, rinsing them afterwards. Using a metal "Kitchen Hammer", beat the breasts flat.
- **:15** Place the breasts laying flat in a shallow baking dish (about 10" x 10" x 2").
  Cover with foil and place in oven. Set timer for 20 minutes. Shred the jack cheese and set aside in bowl.
- **:05** Combine tomatoes, cornstarch, and spices in pan. Cook over medium heat, until thickened (about 3 minutes).
- **:02** Remove dish from oven. Spoon out and dispose of fat. Remove foil and pour sauce over chicken. Top with cheeses; first with parmesan, then the shredded jack cheese.
- **:02** In a large frying pan, heat up 2 tbsp. of water.
- **:01** Add the green beans and cook at medium high heat, covered for about 5 minutes.
- **:04** Place baking dish in oven for 5 minutes, uncovered. Turn off rice - set aside to cool.
- **:01** Green beans are now done.
  Pull chicken out of the oven and top with parsley. Molto Bene!

# Savory Baked Chicken Breasts

**Bread crumbs mixed with the spices give a savory and unique texture to the breasts.   Baked potatoes compliment this dinner very well along with the green beans.**
**Total completion time: 1 hour and 15 minutes**

- ❖ *4 chicken breasts*
- ❖ *¼ cup white wine*
- ❖ *¼ cup plain bread crumbs (can be purchased in enclosed container)*

- ❖ *4 russet potatoes*

- ❖ *1 lb. green beans*

- ❖ *1 tsp. paprika*
- ❖ *1 tsp. dried thyme leaves*
- ❖ *1 tsp. tarragon*

## Minutes

**:05**  Preheat oven to 375°. Proceed to clean chicken breasts, rinsing them off with water; remove chicken skins with paring knife and remove any excess fat that is left on.

**:10**  Line the bottom and sides of a 3-quart oven pan with a large sheet of thick foil. Pour in the wine and add the chicken. Cover with foil.

**:40**  Place in oven for 55 minutes. In a bowl mix the bread crumbs, paprika, thyme leaves, and tarragon and set aside.  While the chicken is cooking in the oven, I use this time to prepare baked potatoes and green beans.

**:02**  Rinse the potatoes well with water. Then, using a fork, poke each potato once on each side. Set potatoes aside on a paper plate.

**:06**  Rinse off the green beans, chop off all tips, and cut to bite size pieces.

**:04**  Place plate of potatoes in the microwave. The plate should be on the edge - not center - of the rotating disc so when they are cooking, heat is evenly distributed. Time for cooking will depend upon size, generally ranging from 8 to 11 minutes, but check them after 8 minutes to see if they are already cooked.

**:02**  Pre-heat a large frying pan with 2 tbsp. of water, bringing the water to boil.

**:01**  Add green beans and cook at high heat with the cover on.  Now check on the potatoes.

**:01**  Remove chicken from oven, remove foil, and spread crumbs evenly. Place back in the oven for five minutes.

**:04**  Check the green beans to make sure water is not fully evaporated. If needed, add another 2 tbsp. of water. Continue cooking at high heat.
Beans are now done and dinner is now complete!

# Spanish Beer Chicken in a Crock Pot

**Beer throws a unique twist into the flavoring that makes it very appealing. This crock pot dinner serves well with brown rice and green beans. Total completion time: 6 hours**

- **3 large chicken breasts**
- **1 pinch salt**
- **1 pinch black pepper**
- **½ tsp. Lawry's® garlic powder**
- **½ tsp. paprika**
- **6 oz. tomato paste**
- **6 oz. beer**

- **4½ - 6 oz. stuffed green olives with the liquid**
- **1 cup Mahatma® brown rice**
- **1 lb. green beans**

- **Kraft ® grated parmesan for flavoring of each individual plate**

**Minutes**

:20    Rinse chicken clean. Cut up chicken into bite sized pieces.

:10    Season chicken with sprinkles of salt, pepper, garlic powder, and paprika.

:05    Put chicken pieces in crock pot. Set on HIGH and cook for ½ hour.

:25    Mix tomato paste with beer and set aside.

4:00    Pour tomato paste mixture and olives with liquid over chicken and reset on LOW. This is now to cook for 5 hours.

:10    Heat up 2½ cups of water to boiling.

:32    Add 1 cup of brown rice and cook for 45 minutes on simmer. This will allow you 5 minutes for the rice to set after it is done cooking.

:11    Rinse off the green beans, chop off all tips, and cut to bite size pieces.

:02    Pre-heat a large frying pan with 2 tbsp. of water.

:03    Add green beans and cook at high heat with the cover on.

:02    Check the green beans to make sure water is not fully evaporated. If needed add another 2 tbsp. of water. Continue cooking at high heat. Remove rice from stove and set aside. <u>Load</u> up that plate with excess amounts of parmesan cheese – it is a fantastic touch for taste buds! Your dinner is now complete!

# Spicy Oven Chicken

This spicy flour mixture adorns the chicken breasts with a tasty and flavorful coating. Potatoes and cauliflower accompany very well.
Total completion time: 1 hour and 20 minutes

- ❖ **4 chicken breasts**
- ❖ **½ cup flour**
- ❖ **3 tbsp. Newman's® Italian Salad dressing**
- ❖ **1 tsp. paprika**
- ❖ **4 tbsp. snipped parsley**
- ❖ **4 tsp. salted butter**

- ❖ **1 medium head of cauliflower**

- ❖ **6 tbsp. water**
- ❖ **4 large potatoes**
- ❖ **¼ cup of salted butter (½ cube)**
- ❖ **2 tblsp. of half-and-half cream**
- ❖ **Salt**

**Minutes**

:05    Preheat oven to 375°. Rinse chicken breasts and remove skins. Place breasts in un-greased 3-quart oven dish. If any breasts are quite fat, slit lengthwise so breasts are opened up and meat cooks fully.

:05    Mix flour, dressing, spices, and butter; blend in water and mix well.

:10    Spread flour mixture evenly over chicken pieces.

:20    Place pan in oven and bake uncovered for 60 minutes. Use this time now to take a short break before starting up the smashed potatoes and steamed cauliflower!

:05    Fill a pot halfway with water and heat up to boiling for the potatoes. Also start up a pot of water to boil for a steamer in order to cook the cauliflower.

:10    Rinse off the potatoes. Then, using a cutting board as your base, peel the potatoes. Cut up into 8 pieces or so per potato - making the potato pieces small in size.

:05    Place the potato pieces into the pot of water. Add about 3 sprinkles of salt. If the water has not yet gotten to boiling, it's alright, just keep the heat on high flame. Simply make sure the potatoes stay fully covered with water while cooking. Allow about ½ an inch from the water to the top of the pan - so there is room for boiling water and it does not overflow onto the stove. When the water is at a full boil, lower the flame a bit while maintaining the boil.

:10    Rinse the cauliflower and cut up for cooking. Place cauliflower in steamer.

:02    Start checking the potatoes by poking with a fork. When the potatoes are quite soft and poke easily, turn off the flame. Drain water out of the pot. Slice the butter into thin slabs and add to the potatoes all over while mixing in with a fork.

:03    Take a break and check the cauliflower. This is generally enough time to cook the cauliflower so it is not too soft. If necessary, cook a little longer.

**Minutes**

**:05** Add half and half cream to the potatoes gradually while mixing in. Now use a stainless steel utensil/potato masher to smash potatoes. (Let this be your opportunity for the day to take out any aggressions or upset your potatoes!!!) Give yourself a little taste to make sure they are buttery enough for you. If so desired, add a bit more and continue mashing.

Put a cover on the potatoes/pan to keep warm. Chicken can now be pulled out of the oven. Cauliflower is cooked by now as are the smashed potatoes.

Process of cooking now being complete - process yourself to eat and enjoy!

# *Thai Chicken in a Crock Pot*

This is another terrific crock pot dinner with a lot of zest using these great spices! A full afternoon is needed for cooking, but actual prep time is only 15 minutes. Calculate time for rice cooking and then work in time for cooking the broccoli.

Total completion time: 5 hours and 30 minutes

- ❖ **3 large chicken breasts**
- ❖ **6 green onions**
- ❖ **14 oz. can coconut milk**
- ❖ **1 tbsp. ginger**
- ❖ **1 pinch dried red pepper flakes**
- ❖ **½ tsp. turmeric**

- ❖ **peanuts**

- ❖ **1 cup Mahatma® brown rice**
- ❖ **2½ cups water**
- ❖ **2 tbsp. cornstarch**
- ❖ **2 tbsp. water**
- ❖ **8 oz. can pineapple chunks**
- ❖ **1 broccoli crown**

## Minutes

**:05**   Rinse chicken breasts and remove skins. Slice in half lengthwise.

**:05**   Chop green onions.

**4:25**   Place chicken breasts in crock pot. Add coconut milk, ginger, pepper flakes, turmeric, and green onions. Cover and cook LOW 5 hours.

**:10**   Preheat pot of 2 ½ cups of water needed for cooking of brown rice.

**:15**   Add brown rice to boiling water and cook assigned 40 minutes (or whatever applies).

**:10**   Rinse broccoli and cut up for cooking.

**:10**   In a small bowl dissolve cornstarch in 2 tbsp. water. Stir in crock pot.
Switch heat on crock pot to HIGH. Add pineapple chunks. Cook for 15 minutes.

**:03**   Preheat frying pan at high heat for 1 minute with 2 tbsp. of water. Add broccoli and cover. Maintain high heat for 5 minutes.

**:02**   Check broccoli to make sure water doesn't fully evaporate. If needed, add another 2 tbsp. of water.

**:05**   Rice is now done. Remove from heat and set aside to cool.  Broccoli is also now done. Dinner is now at completion. Chicken dish serves well poured over rice, topped with peanuts. Broccoli adjoins properly, serving well with butter and parmesan cheese. Enjoy!!

# *Walnut Chicken Strips in a Dry Cooker*

This very tasty dinner is simple to prepare and quite easy to cook, enabling you to slice or chop the vegetables and make a simple salad as the chicken cooks. Using the dry cooker allows you to char the meat, as well as cook fast with much flavor. I have found that serving this meal with barbecue sauce on the side is very popular. In addition to that, a salad and brown rice work well as accompaniments.

**Total completion time: 55 minutes**

- *2½ cups of water*
- *1 cup Mahatma® brown rice*
- *3 small chicken breasts (2.25 - 2.5 lb.)*
- *1 pat of salted butter*
- *2 celery stalks*
- *1 small green bell pepper*
- *5 large mushrooms (when sliced, you'll want to equate 1 cup)*
- *1 small onion*
- *½ cup sliced water chestnuts (4 oz.)*
- *½ cup walnut pieces*
- *Simple salad*

- *KIKKOMAN® Teriyaki Baste & Glaze for flavoring of each individual plate*

**Minutes**

**:05**    Set up a small pot with 2 ½ cups of water for cooking the rice in. Bring to a boil.

**:15**    Add rice to the boiling water. Stir, cover and put to simmer, setting timer for designated time. (The rice I cook takes 45 minutes but your's may take more or less time. Adjust to your time if necessary.)
This time is for preparing a simple salad and then setting aside.

**:12**    Rinse the chicken breasts and remove any skin or fat. Cut into strips about 1 inch thick.

**:03**    Fully coat dry cooker surface with butter. Heat over medium flame with the lid on for 1 to 3 minutes.

**:12**    Place chicken strips on pan and cover with lid. Put on medium-to-high heat and cook about 12 minutes, with alternative shaking of pan every 3 minutes.
Rinse off all vegetables. Proceed to chop celery into 1 inch pieces and thinly slice bell pepper and mushrooms. Cut onion into wedges. Remember to shake pan a few times while the chicken is cooking.

**:03**    Remove chicken from pan, set aside and re-oil pan. Place vegetables in pan, cover, and cook at high flame 5 minutes, shaking a few times.

**:05**    The brown rice would be done at this time. Set aside to cool for 5 minutes.
Add chicken strips, water chestnuts, and walnut pieces to the dry cooker and warm through - about 3 to 5 minutes at medium heat.
Dinner is now done! Flavor chicken strips with teriyaki sauce.

# Chicken Gone Wild!

This wild rice chicken dinner gets well "tamed" in the oven and tastes great with flavoring from chopped onion pieces and cream of mushroom soup. Total completion time: 1 hour and 25 minutes

- ❖ 2¼ cups water
- ❖ 3 small chicken breasts – pre-cooked*
- ❖ 1 small onion
- ❖ 1/3 cup milk
- ❖ 1 pinch salt
- ❖ 2 celery stalks

- ❖ 1 lb. green beans

- ❖ 6 oz. package of long grain & wild rice
- ❖ 10½ oz. Campbell's® Cream of Mushroom Soup

- ❖ Kraft ® grated parmesan for flavoring of each individual plate

**Minutes**

:02  Heat water to boiling.
:03  Cut up chicken to small pieces, removing any fat or skin.
:05  Preheat oven to 350º.
:05  Chop up celery and onion.
:50  Mix all ingredients (except the green beans) in an un-greased 2-quart casserole dish and cover with lid or foil. Bake in oven 50 minutes.
:05  Remove cover and bake uncovered 20 minutes longer.
:08  Rinse off the green beans, chop off all tips, and cut to bite size pieces.
:02  Pre-heat a large frying pan with 2 tbsp. of water, bringing the water to boil.
:03  Add green beans and cook at high heat with the cover on.
:02  Check the green beans to make sure water is not fully evaporated. If needed add another 2 tbsp. of water. Continue cooking at high heat.
     Your dinner is now complete!

*Tip*  Chicken can be pre-cooked in a pot of boiling water. Slice thick breasts lengthwise to equate time needed for cooking chicken pieces (so they are even in thickness). Keep fully doused in water, maintaining boiling state. Cook for 15 minutes.

# *Beef Italiano*

This is a simple and fast cooking stove-top dinner. I found that with the chicken bouillon cube, a mellow tasting twist is added that makes it quite appetizing!
Total completion time: 30 minutes

- *1 cup water*
- *1 red bell pepper*
- *1 green bell pepper*
- *1 medium onion*
- *1 Herb ox® chicken bouillon cube*
- *1 lb. lean ground beef*
- *14½ oz. can Italian stewed tomatoes with liquid*

- *1 lb. green beans*

- *al dente® All-Natural Carba-Nada Egg Fettucine Noodles*

- *½ tsp. basil*
- *½ tsp. dried oregano*
- *¼ tsp. black pepper*

- *Kraft ® grated parmesan for flavoring of each individual plate*

**Minutes**

**:05** Heat 1 cup of water to boiling.
Rinse and cut both bell peppers into small cubes and the onion into wedges.

**:09** Add chicken bouillon cube to the boiling water, stir, and set aside.

**:08** Using a large pot, brown the meat over medium heat. While the meat is browning, use the time to rinse and chop the green beans.

**:01** Spoon excess fat from pan and dispose of it. Add peppers, onion wedges, and tomatoes. Sprinkle basil, oregano, and pepper, and stir in. Cover and return to low heat for 5 minutes. Heat another pot full of water for the pasta.

**:02** Heat a large frying pan with 2 tbsp. of water.

**:02** Add green beans to the frying pan, cover, and cook at high heat for 5 minutes. Place pasta in pot of boiling water and set timer for time needed.

**:03** The main entree is now done. Take off the flame.
Your green beans and pasta are now done!
Go for it!

# *Beef & Noodles in a Dry Cooker*

**Cream of mushroom soup supplies a rich flavored balance to the simple ground beef entree and proves quite appealing to family members.**
**Total completion time: 25 minutes**

- ❖ *1 slab of salted butter*
- ❖ *1 small onion (to equal 1 cup - chopped)*
- ❖ *1 lb. lean ground sirloin beef*
- ❖ *½ tsp. Lawry's® garlic powder*
- ❖ *1 pinch black pepper*
- ❖ *10 3/4 oz. Campbell's® Cream of Mushroom Soup*

- ❖ *1 broccoli crown*

- ❖ *flat egg noodles (cook in 5 to7 minutes)*

- ❖ *Kraft ® grated parmesan for flavoring of each individual plate*

**Minutes**

- **:05**   Rinse and chop broccoli - set aside.
- **:02**   Butter dry cooker and heat with cover on at medium heat for 2 minutes.
  Chop onion.
- **:02**   Add beef to dry cooker. Maintain medium heat to brown. Periodically stir meat to  evenly brown. Spoon out fat as it accumulates.
- **:01**   In a large frying pan place 2 tbsp. of water and bring to boil.
- **:04**   Add broccoli and keep at high heat with cover on.
- **:01**   Check broccoli and make sure water doesn't fully evaporate. If needed, add another 2 tbsp. of water; continue cooking with cover on.
  Preheat pot of water to cook pasta in.
- **:02**   Stir in garlic powder, black pepper, and onion to beef, and cook over medium heat 3 more minutes.
- **:01**   Broccoli is done - remove any water and keep covered to maintain warmth.
- **:01**   Stir soup into beef and cook 3 more minutes.
- **:02**   Add pasta to boiling water - return to boil and set timer.
- **:04**   Entree done.
  Pasta is cooked. Dig in!

# California Pilaf in a Crock Pot

This is a tasty and very easy dinner to make. The fact that it cooks in the crock pot eases you of much time and trouble. Another advantage is the fact that your "accompanying dinner carbohydrate" is the rice cooked right into the recipe! You can use any of the time prior to or during the cooking session to throw together a salad.

I set up this recipe for you to cook at the longest time frame, 5-6 hours - low setting. Another fine point I discovered is the fact that if you are cooking it on low and run a bit behind schedule, it will not affect the food if you leave it cooking for another ½ hour on low.  If you wish to cook it faster overall, you can place the crock pot setting on high and have your recipe cooked in 3 hours.  This recipe cooks in around 6 hours.
Total completion time: 6 hours and 20 minutes

- *2 lb. lean ground beef*
- *1 onion*
- *2½ cups water*
- *20 oz. tomato sauce*
- *2 garlic cloves or ½ tsp. Lawry's® garlic powder*
- *1 cup Uncle Ben's® white rice*
- *Salad*

- *1 pinch salt*
- *1 pinch black pepper*
- *2/3 cup black olives*
- *½ tsp. oregano*

- *Kraft ® grated parmesan for flavoring of each individual plate*

**Minutes**

**:05** In a large saucepan at medium flame, proceed to brown the ground beef, turning over a few times to make sure all beef browns.

**:03** Use this time to chop the onion.

**:04** The beef should now be fully browned. Remove meat from pan without fat and place in crock pot.

**:08** To the crock pan add remaining ingredients: water, tomato sauce, garlic, rice, chopped onion pieces, salt, pepper, black olives, and oregano. Stir well and cover. Designate the setting for 6 hours.

**5:40** Now your recipe is arranged to do its own cooking for close to 6 hours. About 20 minutes before the meal is done, prepare that salad as an accompanying vegetable.

**:20** Prepare salad.
Dinner is now ready!

# *Chili*

It's always fun to have a chili recipe available for barbeques, parties - or just a great family evening bowl. This is my best one to pass on to you.

When you prepare this dinner, make sure you use a very large pot (about 8-quart) to cook in - you will need the space! Something that goes well with the chili is salad. After covering the pot, prepare a salad while your chili simmers. Total completion time: 1 hour and 40 minutes

- ❖ **1 lb. ground beef (preferably lean)**
- ❖ **2 tsp. Lawry's® garlic powder**
- ❖ **1 onion**
- ❖ **1 large can of tomato juice (46 oz.)**
- ❖ **1 large can Italian stewed tomatoes (14 ½ oz.)**
- ❖ **1 tbsp. dried parsley**

- ❖ **1 salad**

- ❖ **Sourdough Bread**

- ❖ **1 tsp. oregano**
- ❖ **¼ tsp. black pepper**
- ❖ **2 tbsp. chili powder**
- ❖ **2 celery stalks**
- ❖ **1 can kidney beans (15 ¼ oz), drained**
- ❖ **1 can black beans (15 ¼ oz), drained**

**Minutes**

:02    Heat the pot on the stove burner over low flame for a moment before adding the ground beef. Stir meat with your cooking spoon so the meat browns evenly. Sprinkle the garlic powder over the meat.

:08    While the meat proceeds to brown, use this time to quickly chop up the onion. Add to the pot. Continue to stir meat occasionally as it browns.

:05    Meat should be fully browned at this point. Spoon excess fat from pot to remove.

:10    Return the pot to the stove, and add juice and tomatoes as well as parsley, oregano, pepper, and chili powder. Raise the heat so as to bring chili to a boil.

:55    Cover the pot and simmer for 1 hour. Use this time now to prepare that delicious salad!

:05    Wash and chop up celery stalks into ½" pieces.

:05    Add celery and beans to chili pot and stir in. Raise heat to bring back to a boil.

:10    Simmer 10 more minutes, covered.
        Dinner is now ready! The chili serves well in big bowls with that sourdough bread.

# *Lasagna*

This recipe is a bit time consuming, but we all love and need a great homemade lasagna recipe to serve and enjoy every once in a while. Here's mine - dig in!
Total completion time: 2 hours and 5 minutes

- ❖ *12 oz. lasagna noodles*
- ❖ *1½ lb. ground beef*
- ❖ *1 can (28 oz) Italian stewed tomatoes*
- ❖ *1 can (12 oz) tomato paste*
- ❖ *1½ tsp. Lawry's® garlic powder*
- ❖ *1½ tsp. oregano leaves*
- ❖ *1 tsp. basil leaves*
- ❖ *16 oz. cottage cheese*

- ❖ *Salad*

- ❖ *1 cup grated Kraft® parmesan cheese*
- ❖ *12 oz. shredded mozzarella cheese*

- ❖ *Kraft ® grated parmesan for flavoring of each individual plate*

**Minutes**
- :01  Set up a large pot of water to boil for cooking of lasagna noodles.
- :10  In a large skillet or pot, brown beef - stirring every once in a while as it cooks.
- :07  The meat should be brown by now. Turn off heat. Drain off the fat.
- :02  Cook lasagna 10 minutes (check the box to verify time, and adjust the time if needed - whether a bit more or less).
- :05  Add tomatoes, tomato paste, garlic powder, oregano leaves, and basil leaves to the pot of meat. Heat to boiling, stirring occasionally.
- :02  Reduce heat and simmer uncovered 20 minutes.
- :01  Place cottage cheese in blender and purée fully - should take about 8-10 minutes.
- :02  Check the pasta and pull off the heat when time is done. Rinse cold water through to make a bit easier for noodle separation.
- :06  The lasagna will need to be sectioned into 3 portions for layering. Let me forewarn you - those pasta noodles are going to be a hassle to handle, separate, and layer. Be prepared to handle with a plastic spatula for separation and realize they may tear a bit. Don't be disappointed - people don't notice! Just make sure the first (bottom) level is fully covered with lasagna noodles.
- :04  Add ½ cup of parmesan cheese to the blender and finish mixing together.
- :05  Set aside ½ cup of the Mozzarella cheese.
- :05  Turn meat skillet off and set aside 1 cup of the meat sauce.

**Minutes**

**:10** In an un-greased 3-quart baking dish, alternate noodles, remaining meat sauce, remaining Mozzarella cheese, and the cottage cheese mixture (all divided in half). Set it up so food is layered as such: pasta, meat sauce, Mozzarella cheese, cottage cheese mixture, pasta, meat sauce, Mozzarella cheese, cottage cheese mixture, and pasta.

**:05** Spread reserved meat sauce over top and sprinkle with ½ cup of Parmesan cheese. Sprinkle reserved Mozzarella cheese evenly across lasagna.

**:45** Place in oven and bake uncovered 45 minutes. Now is the great time to prepare a salad.

**:15** Pull out the lasagna from the oven. Let cool 15 minutes before cutting.
Dig in and enjoy! Sourdough bread will well accompany this one...

# Meaty Halloween Lasagna Casserole

This is a simple and filling dinner to serve a family. It saturates most taste buds quite well, and you have all the food groups included in your ingredients. Begin this dinner with a simple salad.  Total completion time: 1 hour

- ❖ **2 lbs lean ground beef**
- ❖ **salt - a few dashes**
- ❖ **1 pinch black pepper**
- ❖ **1½ tsp. Lawry's® garlic powder**
- ❖ **8 oz. package egg noodles**
- ❖ **5 green onions**
- ❖ **25 oz. tomato sauce**

- ❖ **1 salad**

- ❖ **2 tbsp. salted butter**
- ❖ **8 oz. sharp cheddar cheese**
- ❖ **sour cream for topping**

- ❖ **Kraft ® grated parmesan for flavoring of each individual plate**

**Minutes**

- **:05** Start heating up a pot of water to cook your noodles in.
- **:02** Using a large saucepan, brown the beef (takes about 10 minutes). While doing so, add the salt, pepper, and garlic powder.
- **:03** Add package of egg noodles to that pot of boiling water (it generally cooks in 10 minutes).
- **:02** Chop the green onions and add to the saucepan, mixing in with the meat.
- **:03** Preheat oven to 375º.
- **:02** Spoon the liquid fat out of the saucepan. Add the tomato sauce, stir and heat through over medium heat for 5 minutes.
- **:01** Drain noodles and stir in the butter.
- **:07** Shred the cheddar cheese.
- **:05** In a 3-quart oven dish, layer half the meat, half the noodles, remaining meat, and remaining noodles. Top with cheddar cheese.
- **:30** Place in the oven and bake for 30 minutes. This is now the time for making the dinner salad. Dinner is now complete. This dish serves well with a bit of sour cream spooned on the side of the dinner plate!

# Noodle Casserole

**The multiple layering of this casserole well distributes the cheese to properly flavor remaining ingredients. Total completion time: 1 hour and 10 minutes**

- ❖ *6 oz. package Dutch noodles*
- ❖ *16 oz. cottage cheese*
- ❖ *1½ lbs ground beef*
- ❖ *1 medium onion*
- ❖ *¼ tsp. black pepper*
- ❖ *½ tsp. Lawry's® garlic powder*

- ❖ *1 broccoli crown*

- ❖ *12 oz. can tomato sauce*
- ❖ *8 oz. sharp cheddar cheese*

- ❖ *Kraft ® grated parmesan for flavoring of each individual plate*

**Minutes**

:05    Fill pot with water and set to boil for cooking of noodles.
Place cottage cheese in an electric blender and set on pureé or frappeé.
You will be running it for 5 to 10 minutes, until it is fully smoothed.

:02    Place noodles in pot of boiling water and cook for 8 to 12 minutes (times differ upon the brand at times - set for least time listed on package). Check cottage cheese. If cheese is fully creamed, turn off blender - otherwise continue for another 5 minutes or so.

:03    Preheat large pan. Add the ground beef and start browning the beef at medium high flame, turning beef over as it browns.

:03    Rinse and chop the onion.

:04    Chcck and attend to the noodles. When noodles are cooked, remove from heat and rinse with cold water, fully draining the noodles. Set pot aside.

:08    Beef should be browned by now. Remove from stove and spoon out liquid grease.

:02    Mix in pepper, garlic powder, and tomato sauce with the beef. Simmer 5 minutes.

:03    Rinse and chop broccoli.

:03    Remove meat from heat. Combine creamed cottage cheese and onion with the noodles in a mixing bowl.

:02    Fully shred the cheddar cheese. Preheat oven to 350º.

:05    Using a 3-quart oven dish, layer the ingredients. Place half the beef mixture on the bottom, spreading across. Then place all noodle mixture. Top with remaining half of the beef. Cover beef with cheddar cheese.

:15    Place in oven for 30 minutes.

:07    Rinse off broccoli and cut into bite size pieces.

:03    Heat 2 tbsp. of water in large frying pan to boiling.

:05    Add broccoli pieces. Cook on high heat, covered, for 5 minutes. Add more water if necessary - don't allow pan to get dry.
Dinner is now complete!

# *Tomato Rice Porcupines*

These tasty porcupine meatballs conveniently carry the carbohydrate side of rice built right into their "forms", making dinner preparation that much simpler!
Total completion time: 1 hour and 25 minutes

- ❖ *1 lb. ground beef*
- ❖ *½ cup Uncle Ben's® white rice*
- ❖ *½ cup water*
- ❖ *1 small onion - chopped*
- ❖ *1 dash salt*
- ❖ *½ tsp. celery salt*
- ❖ *½ tsp. Lawry's® garlic powder*
- ❖ *1 pinch black pepper*

- ❖ *1 (15 ounce) can tomato sauce*
- ❖ *1 cup water*
- ❖ *2½ tsp. Lea & Perrin's® Worcestershire Sauce*
- ❖ *1 lb. green beans*

- ❖ *Butter and Kraft Parmesan cheese to flavor beans upon serving*

**Minutes**
- **:05** Chop onion.
- **:10** Mix meat, rice, ½ cup water, onion, salts, garlic powder, and pepper. Using a tablespoon, shape meat mixture into rounded balls. Place them in an un-greased 3-quart baking dish.
- **:10** Preheat oven to 350°.
  Stir together tomato sauce, 1 cup water, and Worcestershire sauce. Pour over meatballs. Cover baking dish with aluminum foil.
- **:42** Bake 45 minutes.
- **:03** Rinse off the green beans, chop off all tips, and cut into bite-size pieces.
- **:05** Remove foil covering baking dish and bake 15 minutes longer.
- **:02** Pre-heat a large frying pan with 2 tbsp. of water, bringing the water to boil.
- **:03** Add green beans and cook at high heat with the cover on.
- **:02** Check the green beans to make sure water is not fully evaporated. If needed, add another 2 tbsp. of water. Continue cooking at high heat.
- **:03** Beans are now done.
  Dinner is complete. Remove casserole from oven.

# *Orientalized Beef*

A truly appealing benefit to the preparation of this dinner is that much of the work involved is simply slicing vegetables and shredding cheese. As a matter of fact, if you wish, you can prepare these vegetables and cheese up to 48 hours ahead of time.  Then store in the refrigerator in individual hole-punched cellophane bags.

In any case, this is a nutritious and tasty meal that is very appealing in appearance because of all the colorful vegetables used. Soy sauce, tomato sauce, and cheddar cheese mix together with browned beef for a unique taste.  I always prepare a simple salad to go with this meal. The salad is generally fixed before starting the meal, then just set it aside.
Total completion time: 33 minutes

- **8 oz. cheddar cheese**
- **6 green onions**
- **3 stalks of celery**
- **1 green bell pepper**
- **1 tomato**
- **½ lb. lean ground beef**
- **5 tbsp. KIKKOMAN® Soy Sauce**

- **8 oz. fresh sliced mushrooms**
- **8 oz. frozen peas**
- **15 oz. tomato sauce**
- **al dente® All-Natural Carba-Nada Egg Fettucine Noodles (takes 5 minutes)**

- **Salad**

**Minutes**

**:05**  Shred the cheese and divide evenly in two portions. Set aside.

**:05**  Rinse off all vegetables. Slice green onions in ½" pieces. Slice celery in 1" pieces.  Slice bell pepper into thin slices. Cut tomato into wedges.

**:06**  Heat up a large pot and brown beef with onions at medium heat. Stir occasionally to brown evenly. Drain out fat.

**:05**  Add celery, mushrooms, and peas to the meat. Stir in the tomato sauce and soy sauce, and cook 4-5 minutes over medium heat, stirring occasionally.

**:02**  Add ½ of the shredded cheese and fully stir in. Set up a pot of water to cook pasta in and heat to boiling.

**:03**  Stir in pepper slices with the meal. Reduce to low heat, cover and completely heat (about 5 minutes).

**:02**  Put pasta in boiling water, return to boil, and set timer.

**:05**  Sprinkle remaining cheese on top of dish. Top with tomato wedges.
Pasta should now be ready. Your yummy dinner is now ready to escort the pasta - Dive in!

# Sirloin Steak Stroganoff

This dinner looks great when served! Using sirloin steak as the meat for the stroganoff gives a rich and tasty twist to this stove-top dish. Spoon servings of sirloin stroganoff over the noodles and have yourself a side of the broccoli topped with butter and grated parmesan cheese.

Total completion time: 48 minutes

- 2 lb. sirloin steak
- ¼ cup salted butter
- 1 can (4 oz.) sliced mushrooms, drained
- 1 small onion
- two 10½ oz. cans beef broth or use 3 Herb ox® beef bouillon cubes dissolved in 20 ounces boiling water
- ¼ cup ketchup
- 1½ tsp. Lawry's® garlic powder
- 8 to 10 oz. package Dutch noodles
- 1/3 cup flour
- 2 cups sour cream
- 1 broccoli crown
- grated Kraft® parmesan cheese

## Minutes

:10   If making the beef broth with bouillon cubes, heat the 20 oz. of water to boiling; dissolve the 3 cubes.

:05   Using sharp steak knife, remove any excess fat layer on the meat. Slice steak into thin strips about 3 inches long.

:02   Preheat a large frying pan and melt butter in the pan. Add the mushrooms and cook for about 5 minutes, stirring occasionally.

:03   Rinse and chop broccoli.

:05   Remove and save the mushrooms. Chop the onion.

:05   Reheat the frying pan and add the sirloin strips. Cook over medium heat while browning the meat.

:02   In another frying pan place 2 tbsp. of water and bring to a boil.

:02   Heat water in a pot to cook the pasta in.

:01   Add broccoli to the frying pan with boiling water and keep at high heat with cover on.

:02   Reserving 2/3 cup of the beef broth, stir in remaining amount while adding chopped onion, catsup, and garlic powder. Cover and simmer 15 minutes.

:02   Add noodles to boiling water and set timer for 9-11 minutes.

:01   Mix together the reserved 2/3 cup of the broth with the flour, then stir it into the meat. Check broccoli to see if a bit more water is needed. Add 2 tbsp. of water if needed.

:01   Broccoli is done. Remove from heat.

:07   Pasta is now ready. Remove and run hot water through. Drain.
Add mushrooms to the pan with the meat; heat to boiling while stirring constantly. Boil and stir 1 minute and add the sour cream. Stir it in over the heat so it heats through.
Dinner is ready to be served!

# *Sirloin Burger Stroganoff*

Ground sirloin steak gives this meal great taste. As a light dinner, it serves very well with the Bok Choy recipe and whole wheat pasta. Because this dinner involves so many cut up vegetables, it works well to simply pre-cut and set aside the vegetables for stove-top cooking.
Total completion time: 40 minutes

## Ingredients for stroganoff

- *4 large mushrooms*
- *½ small onion*
- *1 lb. ground sirloin steak*
- *2 tbsp. white flour*
- *1 pinch salt*
- *½ tsp. Lawry's® garlic powder*
- *1 pinch black pepper*

- *10 ½ oz. Campbell's® Cream of Chicken Soup*
- *8 oz. dairy sour cream*

- *Kraft ® grated parmesan for flavoring of each individual plate*

- *6 oz. whole wheat whole grain pasta*

## Ingredients for vegetables

- *1 head of bok choy*
- *½ cup of bean sprouts*
- *1 broccoli crown*
- *1 large celery stalk*

- *1 large carrot*
- *1 zucchini*
- *1 tsp. KIKKOMAN® Soy Sauce*

- *peanuts to top*

## Minutes
- **:03** Rinse mushrooms and slice. Chop onion. Set these aside to cook with meat later.
- **:03** Rinse bok choy leaves, broccoli, celery stalk, carrot, and zucchini.
- **:06** Chop broccoli and slice celery, carrot, and zucchini. Set aside.
- **:02** Heat a large pan over medium heat for 2 minutes.
- **:08** Add ground beef and start browning while occasionally stirring. Remove excess fat.
- **:05** Stir in flour, salt, garlic powder, pepper, and mushroom slices with meat. Cook 5 minutes, occasionally stirring.
- **:03** Add soup to pan of beef and heat to boiling, stirring constantly.

**Minutes**

**:01**  Reduce meat pan to simmer and cook uncovered 8 minutes.

Fill a pot with water and heat to boiling for cooking of pasta.

Heat a large pan with ½ cup of water to boiling to prepare bok choy and other vegetables in.

**:02**  Place broccoli, celery, carrot, and zucchini in the pan and stir-fry.

**:01**  Add pasta to boiling pot of water and bring water back to a boil. Set timer for 6 minutes (or time designated).

**:01**  Add bok choy and bean sprouts to pan of vegetables and stir in soy sauce.

**:03**  Remove vegetable pan and set aside.

**:01**  Stir sour cream into pan of beef and heat through 2 more minutes.

**:01**  Check pasta. It should be ready now.

Remove dinner. All is ready now!

For delicious extra flavoring, top with peanuts when served.

# *Spaghetti*

Adding tomatoes, bell pepper, and celery does a great job bringing added nutrition from those vegetables into the dinner. The proportions I have given you for spaghetti sauce comfortably accommodates feeding two dinners to a family of four. The sauce keeps well in the refrigerator for up to three days, or in the freezer longer if desired.
Total completion time: 48 minutes

- *2 lb. lean ground beef*
- *1 medium sized onion*
- *¼ tsp. black pepper*
- *1 tsp. oregano*
- *1 tsp. Lawry's® garlic powder*
- *2 cans tomato sauce - 15 oz. each*

- *1 can Italian style tomatoes - 15 oz.*
- *1 green bell pepper*
- *3 stalks of celery*

- *Kraft ® grated parmesan for flavoring of each individual plate*

- *DeCecco® Capellini - slim pasta that cooks in 2 minutes - 8 oz. will feed 4 people*

- *Salad*

**Minutes**

:08    Preheat large 3 quart pot over low heat 2-3 minutes. Place ground beef in pan and begin browning the beef. Every few minutes stir the meat so nothing remains pink or red. Make sure beef does not end up in little tiny pieces - keep a bit of the beef in small chunks!

:05    While keeping an eye on the beef so that it doesn't burn, go on to chop your onion.

:10    Beef should now be brown. Remove pot from the fire and proceed to spoon out the liquid fat. Dispose of this in the sink while running water (you can add a few squirts of dish soap so grease is loosened and doesn't stick to sink).

:05    Return pot to the stove. Before starting up the fire, add black pepper, oregano, and garlic powder. You can adjust these spices based upon how spicy you like your food - the measurements I gave you are fairly mild. Start up stove on low.

:05    Now add tomato sauce and tomatoes. Simmer for 10 minutes with a cover on the pan. Please note that simmering longer can allow spices to blend more and does not overcook the meat. I myself have simmered a pot of spaghetti sauce for up to 30 minutes.
Wash bell pepper and celery sticks. Cut off the top of the bell pepper. Slice in half vertically. Cut out the interior seeds and "frame" from the inside and dispose of them. Then cut into 1-inch vertical slices. Proceed to cut them up into small 1-inch squares.
Cut the ends off of the celery sticks and dispose of them. Then chop celery sticks up into small pieces.

:05    Now get the water boiling to cook the pasta.

**Minutes**

  **:05**  Add vegetables to the sauce, cover again, and simmer for 10 more minutes.
        Use this time now to prepare that salad.

  **:02**  At this point water should be boiling. Place pasta in the pot of boiling water and set kitchen timer for the two minutes.

  **:03**  Pasta is now cooked.
        Spaghetti sauce is completed - dig in!

# *Easy Beef Chuck Mix*

**Here you go red meat lovers!  This beef chuck dish throws in many tasty spices to enjoy, as well as a great sauce to twirl your noodles in. Because it is browned quickly and then simply simmered, the meat comes out real tender! Total completion time: 50 minutes**

- ❖ *2 lb. beef chuck*
- ❖ *1 medium red onion*
- ❖ *1 tbsp. olive oil*
- ❖ *2 tsp. Lawry's® garlic powder*
- ❖ *¾ cup ketchup*
- ❖ *2 tbsp. Lea & Perrin's® Worcestershire Sauce*
- ❖ *2 tsp. paprika*
- ❖ *½ tsp. dry mustard*

- ❖ *Anthony's® egg noodles*

- ❖ *1 lb. green beans*

- ❖ *2 dashes cayenne red pepper*
- ❖ *1½ cups water*
- ❖ *2 tbsp. flour*
- ❖ *¼ cup water*

- ❖ *Kraft ® grated parmesan for flavoring of each individual plate*

## Minutes

:15   Rinse the beef and chop into 2 inch cubes, removing any excess fat.

:01   Slice the onion into thin slices.

:01   Heat olive oil in a large pan.

:08   Add meat cubes and  onion slices. Cook over high heat to brown the meat quickly.  As you cook, stir and mix in the garlic powder.

:03   At this point, the meat should be evenly browned. Stir in the ketchup, Worcestershire sauce, paprika, dry mustard, and cayenne red pepper. Add 1½ cups of water and mix thoroughly.

:06   Cover the pan and leave to simmer for 20 minutes.
Rinse off the green beans, chop off all tips, and cut to bite size pieces.

:01   Heat up another pan for the boiling of your egg noodles.

:02   Pre-heat a large frying pan with 2 tbsp. of water, bringing the water to a boil.

:02   Add green beans and cook at high heat with the cover on.

:01   Add noodles to pot of boiling water. Stir in and bring water back to a boil. These generally take 8 to 10 minutes to cook.

**Minutes**

:02   Mix the flour and ¼ cup of water thoroughly and set aside.

Check the green beans to make sure water is not fully evaporated. If needed, add another 2 tbsp. of water. Continue cooking at high heat.

:05   Turn off the green beans and set aside.

:01   Add the flour mixture to the pan of beef. Heat it over high heat to bring to a boil, stirring constantly. Boil and stir for 1 minute.

:01   Check your noodles to turn off when ready.

:01   Beef is now done.

Dinner is now ready!  Drain the noodles.  Parmesan cheese tops the meal well.

# Pot Roast

You do need the afternoon to prepare this dinner, as pot roast needs 4 hours to reside in the oven. This vintage recipe is, however, well worth the time and effort put out for the tasty rewards it gives. It works beautifully as a serving dish for family get-togethers.

**Total completion time: 4 hours and 10 minutes**

- ❖ **2-3 lb. boneless chuck roast**
- ❖ **3 tbsp. Lea & Perrin's® Worcestershire Sauce**
- ❖ **½ tsp. black pepper**
- ❖ **1½ tsp. Lawry's® garlic powder**
- ❖ **5 carrots - or 12 oz. bag peeled mini carrots**
- ❖ **1 broccoli crown**

- ❖ **small bag boiling onions - about 8-10 oz.**
- ❖ **4 large potatoes**
- ❖ **salt**
- ❖ **¼ cup of salted butter (½ cube)**
- ❖ **2 tblsp. of half-and-half cream**

**Minutes**

:05    Preheat oven to 350º. Rinse chuck roast and, without removing fat, place in a pot roast pan (that comes with a cover).

:05    Fill roasting pan up with water, covering the meat. Add the Worcestershire sauce, pepper, and garlic powder, distributing it evenly on the meat.

:05    Place pan in oven uncovered so as to brown the meat. Set timer for 1 hour.

:55    Peel carrots, chopping off the ends. Cut them in half and then lengthwise, making 6 to 8 carrot strips per carrot. Set them aside for later.

1:55    Add carrots to the pan and return to oven with pan cover on. Set timer for 2 hours.

:05    Pull onions out of bag, remove any loose onion skins, and throw away.

:15    Add onions to the pan and return to oven with cover on. Set timer for 1 hour and get ready to prep for smashed potatoes and broccoli.

:05    Fill a pot halfway with water and heat up to boiling for potatoes.

:10    Rinse off the potatoes. Then, using a cutting board as your base, peel the potatoes. Cut up into 8 pieces or so per potato - making the potato pieces small in size.

:15    Place the potato pieces into the pot of water. Add about 3 sprinkles of salt. If the water has not yet gotten to boiling, it's alright, just keep the heat on high flame. Simply make sure the potatoes stay fully covered with water while cooking. Allow about ½ an inch from the water to the top of the pan - so there is room for water to boil and it does not overflow onto the stove. When the water is at a full boil, lower the flame a bit while maintaining the boil.

:05    Rinse off broccoli and cut to bite size pieces.

**Minutes**

**:02** Start checking the potatoes by poking with a fork. When the potatoes are quite soft and poke easily, turn off the flame. Drain water out of the pot. Slice the salted butter into thin slabs and add to the potatoes all over while mixing in with a fork.

**:03** Heat 2 tbsp. of water in large frying pan to boiling.

**:01** Add broccoli pieces. Cook on high heat, covered, for 5 minutes. Add more water if necessary - don't allow pan to get dry.

**:04** Add half and half cream to the potatoes gradually while mixing in. Now use a stainless steel utensil/potato masher to smash your potatoes. Let this be your opportunity for the day to take out any aggressions or upsets on your potatoes! Smash away!!! Give yourself a little taste to make sure they are buttery enough for you.

Put a cover on the potatoes/pan to keep warm.

Pot Roast Dinner is now ready!!!

# *Sirloin Stew*

This is a tasty version of stew I enjoy because it doesn't take as long as many others I've tried (some taking 2-3 hours). The added peas and bell pepper give it a fresh and unique flavor. When the stew simmers at the end, it is a perfect time to make a salad to accompany your dinner.
Total completion time: 1 hour and 15 minutes

- *2 large sirloin steaks*
- *1 onion*
- *3 medium potatoes*
- *3 tbsp. flour*
- *¼ tsp. black pepper*
- *2 tbsp. olive oil*
- *½ tsp. Lawry's® garlic powder*
- *16 oz. can Italian tomatoes*

- *8 oz. can tomato sauce*
- *1 medium green bell pepper*
- *16 oz. package frozen petite green peas*

- *Kraft ® grated parmesan for flavoring of each individual plate*

- *Salad*

**Minutes**

:10   Rinse steak and cut into 2" x ½" strips, removing excess fat.
:04   Thinly slice onion.
:07   Pare potatoes and cut in half lengthwise, then into 1-inch blocks.
:04   Mix flour and pepper.
:02   Coat meat strips with flour mixture.
:02   Pre-heat pot, adding olive oil after 1 minute.
:04   Add meat strips and evenly brown at medium high flame, turning intermittently.
:04   Rinse bell pepper and cut into ½ inch strips.
:03   Add onion, garlic powder, potatoes, tomatoes, and tomato sauce, and over high flame bring to a boil.
:23   Reduce heat and simmer with cover on, stirring occasionally.
      Prep salad.
:07   Check to see if potatoes are yet tender. If not, cover again and simmer 10 more minutes - then proceed with remainder of recipe. When potatoes are tender, add peas and bell pepper strips.  Heat to boiling with cover off.
:05   Reduce heat. Cook 5 more minutes.
      Dinner is now complete!

# Ham & Scalloped Potatoes in a Crock Pot

This dinner works well within the time frame, because preparation is easy and the remainder of the main course is cooked in the crock pot. The last 20 minutes allows you time to prep green beans.
Total completion time: 8 hours and 30 minutes

- ❖ **4 medium potatoes**
- ❖ **1½ cups cheddar cheese**
- ❖ **1 large white onion**
- ❖ **30 slices of Danola® Premium Sliced Ham, 24 oz. package**

- ❖ **1 lb. green beans**
- ❖ **¼ tsp. salt**
- ❖ **¼ tsp. black pepper**
- ❖ **1 tsp. paprika**
- ❖ **10 oz. Campbell's® Cream of Celery Soup**

**Minutes**

:05     Peel the potatoes.

:05     Shred the cheese.

:15     Thinly slice potatoes and onion, and julienne slice the ham.

:05     Using half of the ham, potatoes, and onion, place a layer of ham, potato slices, and onion slices in the pot. Sprinkle salt and pepper on top. Spread the cheese on top. Again place a layer of the remaining ham, potatoes, and onion. Sprinkle with salt and pepper. Spoon soup over the top. Sprinkle with paprika. Cover the crock pot.

7:42    Set the knob for low and cook for 8 hours. Time passes . . . . . . .

:09     Rinse off the green beans, chop off all tips, and cut to bite-size pieces.

:02     Pre-heat a large frying pan with 2 tbsp. of water, bringing the water to boil.

:02     Add green beans and cook at high heat with the cover on.

:03     Check the green beans to make sure water is not fully evaporated. If needed, add another 2 tbsp. of water. Continue cooking at high heat.

:02     Remove the green beans from heat.
        The crock pot cook time is terminated. Your dinner is now complete!

**Tip**   If you wish, the crock pot can cook on low for up to 10 hours, which allows you to start this meal earlier or cook it later. Another option is also to cook it on high for 4 hours. If that is desired, allow yourself ½ hour prep time, and add the needed 4 hours for cooking time. In other words, to have dinner at 6:00 and cook on high, start full preparation at 1:30.

# *Martian Food*

When I first played with this recipe, I decided to call it Martian Food because the recipe is primarily green in color due to the peas and spinach noodles. It was a name my daughters had a lot of fun with. It always brought about a laugh from their friends when I was questioned about what we were having for dinner, and I would reply from the kitchen "Oh - tonight we're having Martian Food!"

This is one great recipe that is very easy and fast to prepare (a "quickie" that totals 20 minutes start to finish), real nutritious and <u>very</u> green!! It is quite tasty, and really popular with the family! While cooking this meal, I suggest you prepare a simple salad to accompany the entree.

Total completion time: 20 minutes

- ❖ *12 oz. box of Spinach Fettuccine*
- ❖ *12 oz. Danola® Premium Sliced Ham*
- ❖ *4 tbsp. salted butter*
- ❖ *8 oz. can of sliced mushrooms*
- ❖ *1 tsp. Lawry's® garlic powder*

- ❖ *Salad*

- ❖ *¾ cup whipping cream*
- ❖ *16 oz. package frozen peas*
- ❖ *¼ tsp. ground nutmeg*
- ❖ *2 tsp. white flour*

- ❖ *Kraft ® grated parmesan for flavoring of each individual plate*

**Minutes**

:02  On the stovetop, bring a pot of water to boil - in which to cook your Spinach Fettuccine.

:03  Pull out the ham and slice thinly (julienne sliced) into strips.

:01  In a wide pan, melt the butter over medium heat.

:02  At this time, the pot of water should be boiling. Add Fettuccine noodles, return water to boiling and cook for the allotted time - usually 10 to 12 minutes. Stir every once in while so the noodles do not stick. You can make your salad now.

:03  Drain the mushrooms of any water and add them, as well as the garlic and ham, to the pan of melted butter. Cook over medium heat and stir often.

:03  Stir in cream and peas. Bring to a boil over medium high heat, stirring constantly.

:04  Now add nutmeg and white flour. Stir and mix thoroughly, making sure that none of the flour forms lumps. Flour serves the purpose of thickening the sauce. Remove from heat and cover to keep warm.

:02  Check on the pasta now. The noodles should be about ready. Remove from heat and drain. Adding a bit of cold water and draining again can prevent the pasta from sticking. Simply keep the cover on the pan and noodles will maintain warmth. Welcome to a spacey meal of "Martian food" my family always enjoys!
Serve pasta on a plate with a serving of "Martian food" on top. Add parmesan cheese to top it off!

# *Mushgush Quiche Lorraine*

**Cosmetically, this may not be a dinner you will wish to serve guests. Because it tastes so great, however, my family devours this mushgush meal every time!**
**Total completion time: 1 hour and 28 minutes**

* *6 oz. Swiss cheese*
* *½ small onion*
* *6 oz. of low fat Danola® Premium Sliced Ham*
* *1 deep dish pie crust found in frozen foods aisle*

* *1 lb. green beans*

* *3 eggs*
* *¾ cup whipping cream*
* *1 pinch. cayenne red pepper*
* *1 pinch salt*
* *1 pinch black pepper*

**Minutes**

:05   Shred cheese into thin strips, then proceed to mince/chop the onion.

:05   Take the ham slices, stack them and chop into small square pieces.

:05   Preheat oven to 400º and pull pie crust out of your freezer.
Proceed to sprinkle the ham, onion, and cheese pieces into the pie shell.

:03   In a mixing bowl, beat eggs with the whipping cream. Then add the cayenne red pepper as well as salt and black pepper. Mix together and pour into the pie pan. Some pie shells are deeper than others. If you find that there is more liquid mixture than will comfortably fit in, only fill up to the high point.

:60   You can place a piece of heavy foil on your oven rack when baking to catch any overflow from the pan that may occur. Bake in oven 60 minutes.
Rinse off the green beans, chop off end tips and cut beans to bite-size pieces.

:03   Remove pan from oven and let pie stand for 10 minutes before cutting.

:02   Pre-heat a large frying pan with 2 tbsp. of water, bringing the water to a boil.

:03   Add green beans and cook at high heat with the cover on.

:02   Check the green beans to make sure water is not fully evaporated. If needed, add another 2 tbsp. of water. Continue cooking at high heat.
Dinner is now ready!

# *Pasta with Turkey Sausage & Tomatoes*

**Serve turkey sausage over Rotini noodles. Remember that Parmesan cheese is a great topping, a nice topping for both the sausage dinner and the broccoli. Garlic bread accompanies well.**
**Total completion time: 55 minutes**

- ❖ *1 lb. Hillshire Farms® smoked turkey sausage*
- ❖ *1 large onion*
- ❖ *½ tsp. Lawry's® garlic powder*
- ❖ *28 oz. can of Italian tomatoes*
- ❖ *2 tsp. oregano leaves*
- ❖ *1 tsp. thyme*
- ❖ *¼ tsp. black pepper*
- ❖ *1 tbsp. minced parsley leaves*

- ❖ *2 tbsp. ketchup*
- ❖ *Rotini noodles*
- ❖ *1 broccoli crown*

- ❖ *Kraft ® grated parmesan for flavoring of each individual plate*

## Minutes

:20 Remove sausage casings by cutting open both ends of the sausage. Then use a thin sharp knife and insert multiple slits between casing and sausage meat along the length of the sausage to loosen casing. Peel casing off carefully in order to remove less meat. Cut in meat into ½ inch thick pieces.

:10 Heat pan 2 minutes over medium high flame, then add sausages. Cook sausages for 8-10 minutes. Stir every few minutes. Get sausages a nice brown toasted color - but make sure they don't all burn! Use the time that sausages are being browned to peel, slice, and chop the onion.

:05 Add onion and garlic to the pan. Let them cook at medium flame, stirring occasionally for about 5 more minutes.

:03 Stir in tomatoes, spices, and ketchup. Simmer, uncovered, about 20 minutes.

:05 Rinse off broccoli and cut to bite-size pieces.

:04 Set your water boiling to cook the pasta.

:01 Cook the pasta (remember to set that timer so you don't forget to turn off the water!).

:02 Heat 2 tbsp. of water in large frying pan to boiling.

:05 Add broccoli pieces. Cook on high heat, covered, for 5 minutes. Add more water if necessary - don't allow pan to get dry.

Your dinner is now complete! Top with that parmesan cheese!

# Rockfish with Chinese Style Vegetables & Low-Carb Pasta

This fish dinner is rich in taste when cooked with the spices and vegetables. My Chinese Style Vegetable dish and pasta accompany the entree well, and the whole meal is finished in one hour, including prep time!
Total completion time: 1 hour

## Ingredients for Rockfish entree

- 2 large carrots
- 3 stalks of celery
- 6 green onions
- 1½ lb. Rockfish fillets
- 1 pinch salt

- 1 pinch black pepper
- ¼ tsp. paprika
- 1 pinch salt
- 1 tbsp. lemon juice - 1 small lemon

## Ingredients for vegetables and pasta

- ½ head of green cabbage
- 1 green bell pepper
- 2 large celery stalks
- ½ white onion
- ½ tsp. salt

- ¼ tsp. black pepper
- 1 tbsp. KIKKOMAN® Soy Sauce
- al dente® All-Natural Carba-Nada Egg Fettucine Noodles

**Minutes**

:15    Preheat oven to 350°. Rinse carrots, celery, and green onions. Peel and cut carrots into 2" x ½" sticks. Cut celery into ½" pieces. Cut green onions into ½" pieces.

:10    Rinse fish and lay individually in oven dish. Season with ⅛ tsp. salt, pepper, and paprika in Rockfish entree.

:05    Place carrots, celery, and green onions on top of fish and evenly sprinkle ⅛ tsp. salt and lemon juice.

:05    Cover and bake in oven 30 minutes.
Now is your free time to prepare the Chinese style vegetables and pasta!

:10    Rinse off all vegetables. Shred green cabbage. Cut celery into ½" pieces. Chop onion. Cut bell pepper into strips.

:01    In a large skillet heat ½ cup of water to boiling.

:05    Add all chopped vegetables. Cover and cook at high heat for 5 minutes, stirring several times.

:04    Remove any water left. Sprinkle with salt and pepper in the vegetables and pasta section, and mix in soy sauce. Set aside until dinnertime and move on to prepare the low-carb pasta.

:05    Fill a pot with water for cooking of pasta and heat to a boil.
Water should now be boiling. Add the pasta and set timer for 5 minutes (or whatever time the pasta designates). Fish can now be pulled out of oven and dinner is now ready!

# Tuna Circle with Cheese Sauce & Water-Fried Broccoli

The cheese sauce provides a great accompaniment for this Tuna Circle. This inexpensive recipe supplies you with a different route to take in preparing seafood for the family.

Total completion time: 1 hour

## Ingredients for Tuna Circle

- ½ cup chopped onion
- 1 egg
- 2 cans (7 oz. each) Chicken of the Sea® Chunk Light Tuna in water, drained
- ¼ cup snipped parsley
- salted butter
- 1 tsp. celery salt
- ¼ tsp. black pepper
- 2 cups BISQUICK® Baking Mix
- ½ cup water
- 1 tsp. white flour

## Ingredients for Cheese Sauce

- ¼ cup salted butter
- ¼ tsp. black pepper
- 1 cup shredded Cheddar cheese (about 4 oz.)
- ¼ cup BISQUICK® Baking Mix
- 1 pinch salt
- 2 cups milk

- 1 Broccoli crown

## Minutes

:05   Preheat oven to 375°. Chop onion.

:05   Beat egg lightly. Remove 2 tablespoons and set aside.
Stir tuna, onion, parsley, celery salt, and pepper into remaining egg.

:10   Stir baking mix and water well to form a dough; knead a few times, until mixed through, on a board that you first lightly cover with 1 tsp. of flour. Then, using a rolling pin, flatten into a rectangle about 15x10 inches.

:05   Spread tuna mixture on dough. Butter down a cookie sheet.

:05   Beginning at the long side, roll up the tuna rectangle. Placing sealed side down, form the tube into a circle and set on the cookie sheet with the ends joined together.

:05   Using a knife, make cuts ½ of the way through the circle at 2 inch intervals and open up a bit.

:05   Brush top of circle with reserved 2 tablespoons of egg. Place in oven and bake 25 minutes.

:02   Start the cheese sauce. Melt butter over low heat.

**Minutes**

:02 Add baking mix, salt, and pepper. Cook over low heat while mixing.

:01 When bubbling, stir in milk and raise heat to medium.
Heat to boiling, stirring constantly.

:05 Boil and stir 1 minute. Add cheese and mix until melted. Set aside.

:04 Rinse off broccoli and cut to bite size pieces.

:01 Heat 2 tbsp. of water in large frying pan to boiling.

:05 Add broccoli pieces. Cook on high heat, covered, for 5 minutes.  Add more water if necessary - don't allow pan to get dry.
Remove tuna dish from oven. Dinner is now ready!

# Cheesy Corn Tortilla Bake

Minor preparation is involved here - simply shredding cheese and corn tortillas plus slicing of green onions. Primary cooking time is 45 minutes for brown rice while the dinner itself cooks 30 minutes in the oven.
Total completion time: 55 minutes

- ❖ *8 oz. jack cheese*
- ❖ *1 cup Mahatma® brown rice*
- ❖ *2½ cups water*
- ❖ *6 green onions*
- ❖ *8 corn tortillas*

- ❖ *1 cup frozen corn - defrosted*
- ❖ *2 eggs*
- ❖ *1 cup buttermilk*
- ❖ *4 oz. can diced green chili peppers*

- ❖ *1 can barbecued beans*

- ❖ *Salad*

**Minutes**

**:05**  Shred cheese and divide in 2 equal portions.
**:05**  Preheat to boiling the 2½ cups water needed to cook the brown rice.
Preheat oven to 325°.
**:03**  Slice green onions and divide in 2 equal portions.
Check water for rice to be boiling. Start rice.
**:02**  Grease a 2 quart baking dish.
**:02**  Shred corn tortillas into bite size pieces and divide in 2 equal portions.
**:02**  Spread ½ the tortilla bits in base of baking dish.
**:02**  Top with ½ the cheese, ½ the corn, and ½ the green onions.
**:02**  Repeat layering with remaining tortilla bits, cheese, corn, and green onions.
**:02**  Stir together eggs, buttermilk, and chili peppers. Pour over tortillas.
**:15**  Bake 30 minutes uncovered.
Make a simple salad and set aside to serve with dinner.
**:15**  Heat beans.
Serve!

# Crispy Italian Eggplant & Brussels Sprouts

Here's a tasty Italianized dish that appeals to vegetarians, yet gratifies the appetites of meat eaters. Brussels sprouts accompany well.
Total completion time: 50 minutes

- 1 medium eggplant
- salt
- 2 eggs
- 2 tbsp. milk
- ½ cup grated Kraft® parmesan cheese
- ½ cup toasted wheat germ
- 1 tsp. dried basil
- ¼ tsp. black pepper

- meatless spaghetti sauce

- feta cheese

- 1 pat of salted butter
- 1/3 cup of water
- 1 Herb ox® chicken bouillon cube
- 12 Brussels sprouts
- 1 small onion
- al dente® All-Natural Carba-Nada Egg Fettucine Noodles

**Minutes**

:05    Peel eggplant and rinse off.

:05    Thinly slice - ½ inch thick. Place slices on plate and lightly salt. Set aside.

:05    In a shallow bowl, lightly beat together the eggs and milk. In another shallow bowl mix Parmesan cheese, wheat germ, basil, and pepper.
Preheat oven to 400°.

:02    With a pat of soft butter, grease 2 large baking sheets.

:13    Douse each eggplant slice in the egg mixture. Then dip in wheat germ mixture, fully coating both sides. Place in single layer on the baking sheet.

:02    Place sheets in oven and bake, uncovered, 20 minutes.

:01    Fill a pot with 1/3 cup of water. Add bouillon cube and stir in. Bring to a boil.

:07    Peel outer layers of Brussels sprouts, while rinsing off.

:01    Thinly slice onion, separating rings.

:01    Start up a pot of water to cook pasta in. Bring to a boil.

:01    Add Brussels sprouts to pot of chicken bouillon cube water, cover, and bring to a boil. Set timer and cook 5 minutes, while maintaining boil.

:02    Heat spaghetti sauce.

:02    Add pasta to pot of water and cook.

:03    Add onion rings to pot of Brussels sprouts and cook uncovered 3 minutes.
All is now done! Remove Brussels sprouts from stove and pull the eggplant out of the oven. Serve with pasta, feta cheese and sauce.

# *Spinach Soufflé*

I have always enjoyed this entrée because it is quite light, nutritious, and takes only about 15 minutes to prep before putting it in the oven. After that, the recipe does its own thing for an hour, allowing you the freedom and time to prepare a great salad as well as sliced celery sticks and carrot sticks which tie together as tasty and healthy additions!
Total completion time: 1 hour and 15 minutes

- ❖ *8 oz. sharp cheddar cheese*
- ❖ *6 eggs*
- ❖ *6 tbsp. white flour*
- ❖ *16 oz. non-fat cottage cheese*
- ❖ *12 oz. Stouffer's® Spinach Soufflé entree - defrosted*

- ❖ *1 pinch salt*

- ❖ *Salad*

- ❖ *1 pinch black pepper*
- ❖ *1 tbsp. salted butter*

- ❖ *Serve raw carrot sticks and celery sticks as an accompaniment*

**Minutes**

:05   Preheat oven to 350º.

:05   Shred cheddar cheese.

:04   In a large mixing bowl, beat the 6 eggs slightly. Mix in flour, cottage cheese, and  spinach soufflé. Stir in your shredded cheese. Add salt and pepper to season. Cut the butter up into little bits, add to the bowl, and mix thoroughly.

1:01   Fully grease a 3-quart baking dish with butter. For ease, place a slab of butter on a napkin and spread it around. Now pour the mixed soufflé into the dish. Go ahead and place dish into the oven and set the timer for one hour.
During this time, I have found what works well for me is to prepare the dinner salad so it is fully ready for the dinner that is cooked in 1 hour.  Now use the time to chop those carrots and celery sticks…
Timer goes off. Remove your soufflé from the oven and proceed to serve dinner.  Happy dining!

# Springtime Spaghetti

**This dinner has proven popular with adults as well as children and is quite easy to, shall we say, throw together!  Total completion time: 40 minutes**

- ❖ *1 zucchini*
- ❖ *1 lb. broccoli*
- ❖ *1 red bell pepper*
- ❖ *1 green bell pepper*
- ❖ *1 lb. snow pea pods*
- ❖ *½ cup salted butter = 1 cube*
- ❖ *1 cup of half- and- half cream*
- ❖ *1 tbsp. salted butter*

- ❖ *2 tbsp. olive oil*
- ❖ *1½ tsp. Lawry's® garlic powder*
- ❖ *1½ cup of Kraft® grated parmesan cheese*
- ❖ *1 tsp. black pepper for seasoning*
- ❖ *DeCecco® Capellini noodles*
- ❖ *extra parmesan cheese for topping later*

- ❖ *A simple salad accompanies well*

**Minutes**

:10    Wash and prepare a salad and set aside.

:05    Rinse off all your vegetables.

:10    Thinly slice the zucchini. Cut up the broccoli and both bell peppers into small pieces.  Set aside.

:05    Trim ends off the pea pods and set them aside. Start a pot of water heating in which to cook noodles.

:03    In a small pot, heat the ½ cup of butter with the half-and-half cream over a low flame until melted. At the same time you may start cooking vegetables in a large pot. Preheat the large pot for a moment, then add 1 tbsp. butter and 2 tbsp. of olive oil. Heat for 2 minutes, add garlic powder, zucchini, broccoli, and both bell peppers.

:05    Stir-fry over medium heat for 5 minutes. At this time, add the grated parmesan cheese and black pepper to the pot of butter and half-and-half cream, and mix thoroughly with the low flame still on that pot. That should only take about a minute. Then turn off and leave cheese sauce covered.

:02    Add reserved pea pods to the pot of veggies and cook 1 minute. Go over to the pot of boiling water and start cooking the spaghettini noodles.
Drain the noodles. Your meal is now done! Serve the noodles, dish out some sauce on top and mix together. Place vegetables on top and sprinkle added Parmesan.  "Spring" forward and enjoy!

# Vegetables

I've experimented with recipes over the years and discovered something about vegetables that changed my views considerably. I grew up with the idea of boiling a pot of water, placing a colander filled with vegetables over it and then cooking about 20-30 minutes with a cover sealing it in.

After playing around with that idea, I realized I had not enjoyed cooked vegetables as a child, because I'd always found them to be overcooked and at times mushy. Many times they also had been cooked to the point that flavor was missing.

Exploring that a bit further, I learned that overcooking vegetables not only reduces taste, firmness, and texture - but nutrients are also reduced. I proceeded to experiment, and learned some very good ways to cook vegetables. In essence, cooking can be kept simple and use of time decreased. You end up with tastier and more nutritious vegetables. When serving, you can always add toppings of butter, parmesan cheese, salad dressings, spices or any other flavoring to embellish the taste later.

The following recipes show you quick ways I use to cook vegetables. My first recipe uses olive oil. My alternate method, however, uses only a bit of water and maintains a firm texture without overcooking. In addition, less calories and less cleanup!

## *Birds Eye Broccoli Stir-Fry*

### Total completion time: 25 minutes

- ❖ *1 broccoli crown*
- ❖ *2 celery stalks*
- ❖ *1 tsp. olive oil*
- ❖ *8 oz. carrot pieces*

- ❖ *1 red bell pepper*
- ❖ *8 oz. water chestnuts, drained*

- ❖ *1 onion*

### Minutes

:06   Rinse off all vegetables
:10   Cut broccoli and celery to bite-size pieces.
         Thinly slice carrots, bell pepper, and onion.
:01   Preheat large pan.
:01   Add olive oil and heat another minute at medium high heat.
:07   Place separated onion slices in pan and cook at medium high heat.
         Add remaining vegetables. Cover and continue to cook 5 minutes.  Stir and serve!

# Bok Choy

## Total completion time: 12 minutes
- ❖ **1 head of bok choy**
- ❖ **½ cup of bean sprouts**
- ❖ **¼ cup of water**
- ❖ **peanuts to top**
- ❖ **1 zucchini**
- ❖ **1 broccoli crown**
- ❖ **1 large celery stalk**
- ❖ **1 tsp. KIKKOMAN® Soy Sauce**
- ❖ **1 large carrot**

## Minutes
**:02** Rinse bok choy leaves, broccoli, celery stalk, carrot, and zucchini.

**:05** Chop broccoli and slice celery, carrot, and zucchini.

**:01** Heat a large pan with ¼ cup of water to boiling.

**:02** Place broccoli, celery, carrot, and zucchini in the pan, and stir-fry.

**:02** Add bok choy and bean sprouts to pan of vegetables, and stir in soy sauce.
Vegetables are now ready.

# Broccoli

## Total completion time: 15 minutes
- ❖ **1 broccoli crown**
- ❖ **2 tbsp. of water**

## Minutes
**:08** Rinse off and cut to bite-size pieces.

**:02** Heat water in large frying pan to boiling.

**:05** Add broccoli pieces. Cook on high heat 5 minutes with cover on. Add more water if necessary.
Broccoli is now ready.

# Brussels Sprouts

## Total completion time: 20 minutes
- ❖ **1 lb. Brussels sprouts**
- ❖ **1 Herb ox beef bouillon cube**
- ❖ **½ cup water**
- ❖ **1 small onion**

## Minutes
**:08** Rinse off Brussels sprouts, removing outside leaves. Thinly slice onion and separate.

**:02** Heat water in large pan to boiling.

**:05** Mix in bouillon cube. Add Brussels sprouts and cover. Reduce heat and cook 5 minutes.

**:05** Stir in onion slices, separated into rings; cook uncovered for 5 minutes. Add a bit more water if needed.
Brussels sprouts are now ready.

# Brussels Sprouts & Carrots

## Total completion time: 30 minutes

- ❖ *1 lb. Brussels sprouts*
- ❖ *8 oz. carrots*
- ❖ *¼ cup of water*

**Minutes**

- **:05** Rinse off Brussels sprouts, removing outside leaves.
- **:08** Rinse and peel carrot sticks. Then slice in half vertically and then horizontally.
- **:02** Heat water in large frying pan to boiling.
- **:10** Add Brussels sprouts and cover. Reduce heat and cook 10 minutes.
- **:05** Add carrot sticks and cook 5 more minutes covered. Add a bit more water if needed. Vegetables are now ready.

# Green Beans

## Total completion time: 16 minutes

- ❖ *1 lb. green beans*
- ❖ *2 tbsp. of water*

**Minutes**

- **:06** Rinse beans and chop off ends.
- **:04** Heat water in large pan to boiling.
- **:06** Add green beans and cook on high heat 6 minutes with cover on. Add more water if necessary.
  Finished!

# Snow Peas & Carrots

## Total completion time: 21 minutes

- ❖ *12 oz. Snow Peas*
- ❖ *1 lemon*
- ❖ *3 large carrots*
- ❖ *1 tsp. salted butter*
- ❖ *¼ cup of water*

**Minutes**

- **:15** Rinse snow peas and carrots.
  Cut off the ends of the peas.
  Slice carrots about ½ inch thick.
  Squeeze out 3 tsp. of lemon juice.
- **:02** Bring ¼ cup of water to a boil in a large frying pan.
- **:02** Add carrots and boil with cover on for 2 minutes.
- **:02** Add pea pods; cover and boil 2 minutes.
  Remove any water. Mix in butter and lemon juice.

# *Vocabulary*

Baste - to moisten (generally your meats), using a basting brush, every so often brushing with liquid while cooking

Brown - generally refers to cooking the meat to the point where it loses any pink or red color and has turned brown

Casing of sausage - sealant on outside, enclosing the meat

Char - to partially burn

Cum Step Time – total time accumulated at the end of each step while cooking

Dash - (as in a dash of pepper) simply means "a few sprinkles of"

Julienne Sliced - cutting of food into thin strips

Knead - fold, press, and stretch a soft substance such as dough or clay, working it into a smooth uniform mass.

Marinate - to soak in a seasoned liquid

Mince - to chop into small pieces

Pare - to peel/remove outer surface of

Purée - to press (cooked) food through a strainer or food processor

Sauté - to fry lightly in a little fat or oil over medium to high heat

Simmer - to cook at lowest heat to just before reaching boiling point

Step Time – time it takes to complete each step while cooking

# General Cooking Tips

***Bread crumbs*** - Keep a container of prepared bread crumbs on hand in your kitchen cupboard, purchased at the grocery store in plain flavor. They are easy to use in recipes - as opposed to making them yourself. Bread crumbs are also available with different spices and flavors if you so desire.

***Pre-cooked chicken*** - When a recipe calls for chicken, cook for 30 to 60 minutes depending on the size (legs take considerably less than large thighs or breasts). If a recipe asks for chicken to be cut into strips, cook for 20 to 30 minutes. When cooking various chicken pieces at the same time, place larger pieces first and add smaller pieces later as you go along. Once again, allow about 50 to 60 minutes for breasts and large thighs, less for smaller ones, and about 30 minutes for legs.

If a chicken breast is quite thick and large, slit the side to the full length of the breast. This lessens thickness and cooking time. If a recipe calls for cooked chicken pieces that are cut up during preparation, you should cut larger pieces down in size before cooking so they all measure up to about the same size.

Whatever chicken part you are cooking, it is best to remove any skin or fat first (this automatically reduces unnecessary fat content). Take a medium to full sized pot (depending upon the quantity you are cooking), place chicken parts in it and then fill it up with water, about one inch shy of the top of the pot, while keeping your chicken parts submerged in water as they cook.

Bring water to a boil and keep it boiling. Once water starts boiling, lower the flame a bit so the water doesn't boil over. Just keep the water in boiling mode. Also remember that this water in which you have cooked your chicken in can be used as chicken broth afterwards. Usually no more than half a cup to one cup is needed and that is generally more than the amount of broth you have after pre-cooking your chicken. Make sure you remove the layer of fat resting on top.

You can always test tenderness of chicken by stabbing it with a fork. If the fork easily slides in and out, the meat flakes and there is no pink meat, your chicken is cooked. If you pre-cook several days' recipes, chicken can keep fresh in the refrigerator for two additional days before use – otherwise it should be frozen by storing it in a labeled cellophane freezer bag.

*Crock Pot* - Food can be prepared and stored ahead of your meal in a crock pot placed in a refrigerator. Here is a great idea for prepping the night before! Just allow about 30 minutes extra cooking time to make up for low pot temperature caused by the cold refrigerator. I've also found that if cooking on low, adding one-half to one hour does not affect change of cooking - since everything is being cooked so slowly. Don't open a crock pot while cooking. Valuable heat is lost; stirring is not needed and if a pot is uncovered, 15 to 20 added minutes are needed to regain lost heat.

*Defrosting* - When defrosting meat for cooking, allow it to set about 48 hours in the refrigerator (transition from freezer to refrigerator). If you are in a bind and find that you need to cook some meat the same day but, if it is frozen, you can resort to a microwave. Open the cellophane bag it is stored in or place the meat on a paper towel on the microwave disc, and set the microwave to 'defrost'. Generally allow meat 15 to 25 minutes to defrost. Just check on it by poking a fork into the meat. If the fork slides in and out easily, your meat can be pulled out. Just make sure you don't leave it in excess time or you will start cooking the meat - disrupting your timed recipe steps.

*Eggs Hard Boiled* - Fill pan with water to the point that eggs are fully immersed. Bring water to a boil. Set timer for 5 minutes and maintain boiling water (but maybe lower the heat a bit so boiling continues and water does not spill out - causing you unnecessary cleanup...). After 5 minutes turn off the heat and remove the eggs from hot water. This will deliver hard boiled eggs at a nice yellow/orange color. If you prefer hard-boiled egg yolks not as tender and at a lighter yellow color, set timer at 6 minutes. Also, if I may suggest, it is no fun checking out your eggs in the refrigerator and not being able to tell which are hard boiled! A foolproof way I have always used to identify hard-boiled eggs is to mark the egg shell at both ends with a penciled "X" mark. The marking does not go through the shell to the egg itself, but informs you which eggs are hard-boiled in the refrigerator.

*Eggs – Omelets* - Decide if you simply want to cook a plain omelet, or if you want to include additional ingredients (i.e.: cheese or chopped onions). If you do want to add ingredients to your omelet, take time beforehand to shred or chop what you desire to add. A small amount will add enough to an omelet for one person. Crack two eggs over a mixing bowl. Beat thoroughly with a fork, adding salt and pepper if so desired. Pre-heat a frying pan about one minute, then lightly butter. Pour in the eggs. Cook over low to medium heat. The eggs will begin to solidify at a point closest to heat in the center of the pan, with the inside layer staying a bit wet. At this time you can either use a spatula to fold over one half of the egg layer over the other (forming half a circle) or you can add ingredients prepared earlier include in your omelet. Two more minutes or so and your omelet is done!

*Eggs – Scrambled* - Crack eggs over a small bowl. Add about 1 tsp. of milk per egg and thoroughly mix. Add salt and pepper and stir in. Pre-heat a frying pan about a minute, then lightly butter. When butter is melted, pour in eggs. Keep heat at medium and scramble the eggs as they cook. They are done when consistency becomes solid, still wet, but not overcooked. This generally occurs in 3 to 4 minutes. Turn off the heat 15 to 30 seconds before you remove the eggs from the pan.

*Freezer* - Store individual foods for recipes (i.e.: pre-cooked chicken). Use freezer-type plastic bags and label with date, type, and amount of food.

*Garlic Powder* - This should be kept on hand. Buy coarsely ground garlic powder - not garlic salt. This can be used for all sorts of recipes as a fresh garlic substitute. ¼ teaspoon equals 1 medium garlic clove. Garlic powder is sold in plastic containers in the spice section. Once you open a container of garlic powder, store it in the refrigerator to retain freshness. It is also very handy for use in making garlic bread!

*Lettuce* - Lettuce can be cleaned and stored ahead of time for salad. After washing lettuce, shake off excess water, place in a cellophane storage bag, seal tightly, and punch several holes in the bag to let water vaporize out. Lettuce can be stored in the refrigerator for two more days and stay fresh. This works well if you eat salad often. Just do a large washing and cleaning of lettuce on day 1 - and you can be covered through day 3. This same idea can apply to vegetables you use to decorate your salad. I've found it best to keep veggies in separate bags when storing them this way. It saves you some time . . .

*Microwave Defrosting* - Remove food from package beforehand - don't use foam trays or plastic wraps. Cook meats immediately after defrosting in a microwave oven, because areas of frozen meat may actually cook during defrost. Don't use partially cooked meat later.

*Microwave Reheating* - Cover foods with lid or microwave safe plastic wrap to hold in moisture and provide safe and even heating.

*Microwave Containers* - Glass, ceramic containers, and all plastics should have labels indicating they are safe for microwave oven use. Plastic storage containers (i.e., like those with purchased margarine), take out containers, and other one-time use containers should not be used. They can warp or melt and chemicals can migrate into food. Microwave plastic wraps, wax paper, paper plates, cooking bags, parchment paper, and white microwave safe paper towels should be safe to use.

Don't let plastic wrap touch foods during microwave cooking. Never use thin plastic storage bags, plastic grocery bags, newspapers, or aluminum foil in a microwave oven.

*Onions* - When preparing onions for cooking or serving, cut off a thin slice from the top and bottom to expose the onion. Then go on to peel the outer layer of protective skin on the outside of the onion. When you use onion rings in a recipe, or to top hamburgers, you can slice them very thin. Otherwise, keep your slices slightly chunky and go on to chop them up after slicing in order to obtain chopped onion pieces. If you are quite sensitive to working with onions (eyes tear up easily), store your onions in the refrigerator after you return from the store. Your eyes will not tear up as quickly if you use cold onions. Onions can stay fresh two more days in a refrigerator after being prepared - cellophane bag or cover - holes punched in for air to pass through so no moisture develops and "sits" on vegetables. This way quality or freshness doesn't spoil.

*Pasta* - Low-carb pasta is now available. It tastes quite good, is lighter in consistency, and calorie/carbohydrate content is much lower. Add a slab of salted butter or tsp. of cooking oil to water so pasta doesn't stick together. When done, run under hot, not cold water before draining to avoid stickiness.

*Potatoes Baked* - Potatoes can be cooked in a microwave and save you a bunch of time. Scrub your potatoes and poke a few holes with a fork on both sides. Place potatoes on a paper towel in the microwave on the side, not the middle (so they rotate evenly on the microwave plate), and cook for 10 to16 minutes - depending on potato size and how soft you want them. You can cook up to four at a time. If you put in more potatoes, you will need more time.
Baked potatoes in a crock pot need to be rinsed and damp with a few holes poked in. Cook on low 6 to 8 hours.

*Potatoes Layered Cheese* - Wash and scrub about five medium-size potatoes. Slice into about ½ inch slices. Set the slices in a steamer over boiling water. Steam about 10 to 13 minutes. Start checking your potatoes, poking them with a fork to determine softness. Make <u>sure</u> they don't get mushy - only gently cooked. Remove with a spatula and layer in an oven-safe dish. Place one layer of potato slices in the dish, butter lightly, then lightly sprinkle over all with grated parmesan cheese. Place another layer of potatoes in the dish, butter and sprinkle cheese. Repeat until you run out of potato slices! For the top layer, you can either finish off with another sprinkle of parmesan cheese, or shred about four to six ounces of jack cheese and sprinkle it on top. Melting cheese into this dish makes it very tasty and appealing. Also, using cheddar or other types of cheese helps the potatoes fit well with whatever dish you choose and enhances any preferences you have for cheese flavors. Heat in 375° oven about ten minutes.

*Potatoes Smashed* - Wash and peel four medium-size potatoes. Cut each potato into about 10 pieces. Put in a pot and fill with enough water to just cover the potatoes. Sprinkle ½ tsp. salt.  Bring water to a boil. Cook potatoes, maintaining the boil, uncovered. After about 12 to 15 minutes, start checking your potatoes, and poke with a fork to determine softness. When desired softness is obtained, turn off heat and drain the potatoes. Add eight slices (¼ cup or ½ a cube) of salted butter. Mix and mash. Then slowly add dairy half-and-half cream or whipping cream, about ⅛ cup or 2 tblsp.  Continue to mash until thoroughly mixed. Add more butter or cream if needed or desired.

*Pre-cook* - At times I use another manner in which to provide pre-cooked chicken for various additional recipes. When cooking Intoxicated Chicken, at times I prepare a larger amount than shown in the recipe.  Leftovers can then be used in other recipes. The "intoxicated" chicken has a very mild flavor that does not interfere with existing tastes found in other recipes.

*Preheat* - Preheat  pans at low heat 1-2 minutes on your stovetop before oiling or buttering for cooking. It makes for less likelihood of food sticking - as well as easier cleanup afterwards.

## Safety Precautions  when cooking:
- Always keep oven mitts on hand and don't underestimate the heat of ovens or stoves.
- Use placemats for hot dishware when removing it from stove or oven.
- When you place pots or pans on the stove, make sure handles do not extend past your hand, because you can knock hot cookware off the stove and all over yourself (or kids if any are around) if you are rushing or just inattentive.

*Salads* - Salads can stay fresh two more days in a refrigerator after being prepared. Punch holes in a cellophane bag or cover to breathe so moisture sitting on vegetables will not spoil quality or freshness. Salads served with a meal do provide an added and appealing avenue of nutrition to a dinner.  I believe in "adorning" the lettuce with numerous "colorful" additions. Using green onions, celery and radishes top the list for easy preparation and colorful accompaniment.  Red and/or green bell peppers are also a popular choice. Shredded jack cheese proves to be a popular embellishment. The cheese is also something that you can shred an extra amount of to be refrigerated and stored in a cellophane bag for future use in the next few days.

*Sauces* - If you have a recipe cooking on the stovetop and the darn sauce doesn't seem to want to thicken up, you can add some corn starch or flour. Just add about ½ a teaspoon, stirring well. Add a little bit more if you need to, mixing well as you go along to make sure the corn starch or flour doesn't clump up anywhere.

*Soup Broths* - When a chicken or beef broth is needed in a recipe, bouillon cubes are a fine and quicker replacement for the recipe as opposed to creating a fresh soup just for broth. Use one bouillon cube or packet for every cup of hot water.

*Sour Cream* - Sour cream makes a tasty topping for baked potatoes, but if you do not to have any at home, try what I have used on many occasions - plain yogurt. Plain low fat yogurt makes a fine replacement for sour cream and tends to be less fatty and lower in calories.

*Spices* - Let me share my list of on-hand spices with you. They keep for long periods and supply great seasoning for recipes or individual meal servings. I have a spice tray on the kitchen counter, where I keep my main supply. Get yourself an attractive spice tray that will also serve as a decoration on your counter. These are my main spices: Basil, Bay Leaves, Java Cracked Black Pepper, Cayenne Pepper, Celery Salt, Chili Powder, Curry Powder, Marjoram Leaves, Ground Mustard, Ground Nutmeg, Paprika, Crushed Red Pepper, Sage, Sesame Seeds, Tarragon leaves, Thyme leaves. Others that are kept in the cupboard are: Ground Cumin, Ground Cinnamon, Garam Masala, Ground Ginger. Here are some kitchen regulars that can be purchased in large quantities: Black Pepper, Garlic Powder, Oregano Leaves, Parsley Flakes, Salt, and Sugar.

*Vegetables* - Always rinse well before using. Cut off stems, tips, or inner seeds on veggies such as: bell peppers, broccoli, carrots, celery, green beans, green onions, and radishes. Pre-cut onions and store them in the refrigerator in cellophane, hole-punched bags for up to two extra days. Punching holes in the bags keeps moisture from setting in and decomposing the vegetables. Whatever moisture is still in the vegetables can evaporate. Pre-cut vegetables will generally keep two extra days. When stir-frying in the pan with water, time span can be longer to char/brown the vegetable for tasty variation. Keep an eye on it the first time, as different stoves can provide different temperatures.

# General Equivalents

| |
|---|
| Dash or a pinch = 1/8 tsp. |
| 3 tsp. = 1 tbsp. = 15 ml. |
| 2 tbs. = 1/8 cup |
| 4 tbs. = ¼ cup |
| 16 tbs. = 1 cup |
| 5 tbs. + 1 tsp. = 1/3 cup |
| 4 oz. = ½ cup |
| 8 oz. = 1 cup |
| 16 fl. oz. = 2 cups = 1 pint = 1 lb. |
| 1 oz. = 2 tbs. - fat or liquid |
| 1 cup of liquid = ½ pt. |
| 2 cups = 1 pt. |
| 32 fl. oz. = 1 quart = 4 cups = 2  pints |

# Kitchen Equivalents

| | tsp. | tbs. | fluid ounce | gill | cup | pint | quart | gallon |
|---|---|---|---|---|---|---|---|---|
| 1 teaspoon = | 1 | 1/3 | 1/6 | 1/24 | --- | --- | --- | --- |
| 1 tablespoon = | 3 | 1 | ½ | 1/8 | 1/16 | | | |
| 1 fluid ounce = | 6 | 2 | 1 | ¼ | 1/8 | 1/16 | --- | --- |
| 1 gill = | 24 | 8 | 4 | 1 | ½ | ¼ | 1/8 | --- |
| 1 cup = | 48 | 16 | 8 | 2 | 1 | ½ | ¼ | 1/16 |
| 1 pint = | 96 | 32 | 16 | 4 | 2 | 1 | ½ | 1/8 |
| 1 quart = | 192 | 64 | 32 | 8 | 4 | 2 | 1 | ¼ |
| 1 gallon = | 768 | 256 | 128 | 32 | 16 | 8 | 4 | 1 |

# Miscellaneous Equivalents

| |
|---|
| 1 pinch =1/8 teaspoon |
| 1 teaspoon = 60 drops |

# Pot Sizes

| |
|---|
| 48-oz. (6 cups) is good for cooking soup or rice |
| 2-quart (8 cups) |
| 3 ½ -quart for spaghetti |
| 8-quart for chili |

# Bulk Purchases

If you have room in your home to store non-perishable items, take advantage of membership grocery stores where you can buy in bulk. Many non-perishable items can be purchased and stored in large numbers, and you will find the amount of money you save really adds up.

Items falling into this category include canned goods such as: tomato sauce, tomatoes, tomato paste, soups, vegetables, and tuna. These can generally be found in packs of six or eight cans. Rice and various types of pasta are also available, as well as many foods in the freezer section. Bottled or canned beverages are also a good item to stock up on if used. Cleaning agents, bathroom toiletries, cellophane wrap, foil, napkins, paper plates and cups, paper towels, sandwich bags, storage bags, tissues, toilet paper, and wax paper should also be purchased in bulk to save money.

Cereals, peanut butter, jams, condiments (ketchup, mustard, salad dressings, and spices), cooking oils, shortening, and vinegar can also be purchased at these stores. Purchase in bulk quantities for a party.

When grocery shopping is done, keep an eye out for buying poultry in bulk packages. Chicken legs and thighs, as well as breasts, can be purchased in packages of six to ten per tray and you do save a large amount on the price. What can be done with this is that you pull out dinner size portions of the chicken and separate them in sealed cellophane bags (if cooking for a family of four, supply enough meat for one dinner). Label each bag with the date as well as identifying quantity and type of meat (i.e.12/02/07 - 4 chicken breasts). Store the bags in the freezer. In this way you can keep food fresh and readily available. Microwave defrosting will come in handy later.

You can save money when you buy meats that are purchased by the pound, as opposed to being pre-packaged. For example, if you buy ground beef already packaged, many times it is ¼ to⅓ of a pound more (as in 1.23 lb). If your recipe only calls for 1 lb., that extra amount will prove to be an unneeded excess. Just have the butcher weigh meat for you and package it. Those few minutes you spend will save you time that does add up, and no food or money gets wasted.

# Sample Kitchen Supply/Grocery Checklist Options

__ice __ice cream cones
__bell pepper __celery __ potatoes
__boiling onions __cucumber __radishes
__bok choy __eggplant
__broccoli __green beans
__romaine lettuce

__Brussels sprouts __green onions
__snow pea pods __cabbage- green
__mushroom __soy beans
__cabbage- red __onions __sprouts
__carrots __parsley __tomatoes
__cauliflower __zucchini

__melon __lemon __nectarines
__manderine oranges __grapes
__peaches __strawberries __bananas
__red delicious apples

__health foods __peanut butter bars
__toys __stationary

__popcorn - fat free __trailmix
__Spanish peanuts

__hand soap __lotions __liquid hand soap
__shower caps __razorblades
__razors __sunlotion __shampoo
__conditioner __hair spray __polish remover

__nasal decongestant __Cough Syrup
__vitamins A-Zinc
__antacid – regular __aspirin __Toothpaste
__ waxed dental floss __deodorant
__tampons/pads

__chapstick for dry lips __vaseline
__calamine lotion
__band-aids __cotton balls __rubbing alcohol
__hydrogen peroxide __sewing goods

__beer __white wine __red wine

__Smoked turkey __Salami __ham __hot dogs

__cheddar cheese __string cheese
__Swiss cheese __jack cheese
__cream cheese __tortellini __feta cheese

__cleaning products __non-detergent ammonia
__plastic gloves__ scouring pads
__soap scum remover __bleach
__ mildew remover __sponges__ detergent
__mop sponge __dish soap __dishwasher soap

__toilet paper__ paper towels
__ napkins __matches
__ trash bags __baggies __cellophane wrap
__facial tissue __paper plates __foil
__toothpicks

__soft drinks __snack mix __peanuts
__corn chips __almonds __sourdough pretzels
__cocktail peanuts __nuts

__flavored teas __soft drinks __sports drinks
__glass fruit drinks __frozen fruit drinks
__water __sparkling water

__ crackers __cookies __candy
__marshmallows

__breadcrumbs __flour
__baking soda __salt __pepper
__garlic powder __spices __corn oil
__olive oil __walnuts
__shortening __sugar __barley
__parmesan cheese __dry beans
__spaghetti sauce
__chili sauce __brown rice
__white rice __couscous
__low-carb pasta __green noodles
__twirly noodles
__Dutch flat noodles __Capelline (2 min.)
__eggs __butter-salted
__cottage cheese __buttermilk
__half &half __whipping cream
__nonfat milk __yogurt
__cream cheese

__veg. stir fry w/chestnuts __soy sauce
__mushrooms __tuna
__macaroni & cheese
__soups: __vegetable __split pea w/ham
__tomato __chicken noodle
__cream of mushroom __celery
__chicken __chicken broth __broccoli cheese

## Grocery Options (cont.)

__green beans __kidney beans __picante sauce
__bouillon cubes __french fried onions
__water chestnuts __olives
__stuffed olives __croutons __mustard
__Olive sauce __mayonnaise __Italian light
__Italian dressing __barley
__balsamic vinegar __ketchup
__Worcestershire® sauce __salad dressing
__barbeque sauce __steakhouse marinade
__teriyaki sauce

__sourdough bread __wheat bread
__sourdough roll __buttermilk bread
__English muffins __wheat bagels
__hot dog buns __grape jelly __raisins
__apricot preserves __spun honey
__peanut butter __smooth __nutty
__regular coffee __decaf coffee
__#2 coffee filters __various teas
__cocoa __toasted wheat germ __applesauce
__granola __cornflakes __oatmeal
__ other cereals
__Hershey's® syrup __molasses
__tomato juice __fruit juice
__ice cream __ice cream topping
__pie crust

__frozen foods __peas __corn__ pizza __ravioli
__stir fry veg w/ chestnuts __orange juice
__mixed vegetables __macaroni & cheese
__spinach soufflé

__chewing gum __stamps

**List Main Entrée Items:**

__ chicken __ beef ___ fish ___etc.

## Specific Ingredients Used and Chosen for Recipes

**Al Dente® All-Natural Carba-Nada Egg Fettuccini Noodles**
**Al Dente® Spinach Fettuccine Noodles**
**Anthony's® Egg Noodles**
**Barilla® Farfelle Bowtie Noodles**
**Bisquick® Baking Mix**
**Bradshaw's® Spun Premium Honey**
**Campbell's® Cream of Celery Soup**
**Campbell's® Cream of Chicken Soup**
**Campbell's® Cream of Mushroom Soup**
**Chicken of the Sea® Chunk Light Tuna**
**Danola® Premium Sliced Ham**
**DeCecco® #93 Rotini Corkscrew Noodles**
**Del Monte® Apricots**
**Durkee's® French Fried Onion**
**Garam Masala® Indian Seasoning Powder**
**Herb Ox® Bouillon Cubes**
**Hillshire Farms® Turkey Smoked Sausage**
**Hunt's® Tomato Sauce**
**Kellogg's® Cornflakes Cereal**
**Kikkoman® Soy Sauce**
**Kikkoman® Teriyaki Baste & Glaze**
**Kraft® Parmesan Cheese**
**Lawry's® Garlic Powder**
**Lea & Perrin's® Worcestershire Sauce**
**Mahatma® Brown Rice**
**Manzanilla® Whole Green Olives**
**Mrs. DASH® Salt Free Original Blend Seasoning**
**Newman's Own® Olive Oil & Vinegar Dressing**
**Progresso® Plain Bread Crumbs**
**S & W® Italian Stewed Tomatoes**
**Star® Spanish Olives**
**Stouffer's® Spinach Soufflé**
**Uncle Ben's® White Rice**

# *Necessary Kitchen Tools for Cooking and Serving*

bottle opener
can opener
cork pull
cutting boards
garlic press
meat thermometer
nutcracker
timer
mixing bowls
colander
full size measuring cup-accommodating
> 4 cups (preferably glass to handle any
> hot temperature)

grater
ice cream scooper
ladle
large serving spoons
measuring spoons
metal hammer to flatten meats
peeler
rolling pin
spatula
whisk
basting brush
metal hand-held potato masher
clippers for removing and serving foods
scrubber for scrubbing potatoes prior to baking them

coffee maker
electric blender
food processor
toaster or toaster oven

# *Kitchen Tools (cont.)*

salad spinner to quick dry lettuce
knives:
>3.5" paring
>5" utility
>8" chef
>8" slicer

large cookie sheet
6" aluminum round dish - for pies
crock pot - 6 quart to cook and serve
6" frying pan - non-stick
10" frying pan - non-stick
11" griddle - non-stick (for pancakes)
roaster with cover
roasting rack
steamer basket

various oven proof pans for baking, roasting and cooking -
>2 & 3 quart - with covers

1 quart saucepan
2 quart saucepan
1½ quart pot
3 quart pot with steamer
8 quart pot

tea kettle (a whistling one is handier to
>inform you when water is boiling)

apron
oven mitts
dish rack / drainer
dish sponges (clean or replace often due to bacteria buildup)
plastic hand gloves
dish towels

# Kitchen Tools (cont.)

large cleaning sponges
butter dish
coasters
napkin holder
salt/pepper shakers
spice rack
placemats

salad bowl for serving

daily dishware set with coffee cups
practical drinking-ware for daily use
silverware
steak knife set
sugar cup with cover
plastic storage-ware sets with covers
2½ quart juice jar/server

# Chinaware

serving platter
wine glasses
beverage glasses
sugar cup

glass or ceramic cookware that is oven and microwave proof:
       1¾ cup
       1 liter
       1.5 liter
2 quart  8x8x2"
3 quart 13x9x2"
4 liter oval with glass cover

# Disposable Necessities

wax paper
napkins
disposable plates
disposable cups
Styrofoam cups for coffee
cellophane wrap
aluminum foil
sandwich bags
quart size freezer bags
coffee filters
bag clips to keep opened bags shut

# *Source Information*

These complete meals have been cooked for my family for many years. Some entrée recipes are original and some have been passed down from the family. Other recipes and derivative recipe sources are unknown, but the ones that are known are referenced in the text below. Every meal offered has not only the entrée, but also side orders adjoined in a manner that I have found work best for a tasty and embellishing preparation of what is being served.

PAGE SOURCE

| | |
|---|---|
| 34 | Derivative of 101+ Recipes, Lemon Honey Chicken |
| 37 | Derivative of 101+ Hurry Chicken Recipes, Quick Italian Chicken |
| 15 | Attributed to 101+ Hurry Chicken Recipes, Apricot Chicken Noodle |
| 42 | Attributed to Mable Hoffman's Crockery, Thai Chicken |
| 73 | Attributed to Better Homes & Garden® Vegetarian, Crispy Italian Eggplant |
| 55 | Derivative of '71 Betty Crocker®, Sirloin Steak Stroganoff |
| 60 | Derivative of '71 Betty Crocker®, Easy Beef Chuck Mix |
| 53 | Attributed to '71 Betty Crocker®, Tomato Rice Porcupines |
| 70 | Attributed to '71 Betty Crocker®, Tuna Ring Circle with Cheese Sauce |
| 56 | Attributed to '71 Betty Crocker®, Sirloin Burger Stroganoff |
| 66 | Derivative of Sunset® Quick Meals With Fresh Foods, Martian Food |
| 35 | Attributed to Sunset ® Quick Meals With Fresh Foods, Orange Bunny Chicken |
| 40 | Attributed to Better Homes & Garden® Dieter's Cookbook, Spicy Oven Chicken |

# Recipe Index

# About the Author

Alicia Reynolds is a happily married homemaker who has raised two college-age daughters in Southern California.

Exercise rates high on her list of interests.  She regularly participates in classes for body sculpting and body conditioning as well as mat Pilates.  Roller blading on the bike path at the beach with her husband is another one of her enjoyments. This all attributes to maintaining a healthy and fit body.

She receives pleasure in reading biographies, non-fiction books and solving puzzles.

Her fervor for preparing meals has cooked up smiley faces from the whole family over many years.  Enthusiastically-prepared dinners for family and friends have produced millions of happy taste buds!

Made in the USA
Charleston, SC
05 May 2010